LISTENING IN THE REAL WORLD
Clues to English Conversation

Michael A. Rost
and
Robert K. Stratton

LINGUAL HOUSE

Longman Group UK Limited,
Longman House, Burnt Mill, Harlow,
Essex CM20 2JE, England
and Associated Companies throughout the world.

First printing, 1978
Third impression 1991

Produced by Longman Group (FE) Ltd.
Printed in Hong Kong

ISBN : 0 940 26400 5

Acknowledgements

Our thanks to George M. Landon for his suggestions and editing.
Our appreciation to Don Doucette, Mary Jo Hilpert, Kathy McGrath,
and Emily Wagner for their help in producing the tapes.

Cover and Text Design	Michael P. Sidorak
Tape Production	Paul R. Estes

Introduction

Listening in the Real World: Clues to English Conversation has been designed to bridge the gap between the formally enunciated language of the ESL classroom and the informal language that the student is likely to encounter beyond the classroom setting. By concentrating on a series of commonly spoken reductions, the tape-text attempts to make English comprehensible to the ESL student who may have formulated an inaccurate set of expectancies about the way English should sound. The thirty-six lessons of the book are intended to help the student decipher the real world English of reduced forms (assimilations, coarticulations, and glides). The tape-text gives the English language learner practice in listening to and repeating sentences as they are likely to be spoken by a native American speaker of English. The lessons are arranged in a cumulative fashion so that reductions presented in earlier lessons are incorporated in later lessons.

The text has not included all the reduced variations of English that the student might encounter in the language. The emphasis has been placed on commonly spoken reductions. To aid the student who may not be familiar with formal phonetic systems, all reduced forms have been written in the Roman alphabet.

Listening in the Real World is divided into three parts: 1) a set of thirty-six ordered reduction presentations, 2) a set of two hundred situational dialogs, and 3) a set of two hundred activation exercises based on the dialogs. The tape-text may be used in several ways. For more advanced students, the teacher may want to begin with Part Two, the dialogs, and work on the reduction patterns in Part One as the need arises. For intermediate students, it is suggested that the teacher begin with Part One, the presentation lessons, and have the students repeat the set of reductions contained in each lesson. Following the presentation exercises, there is a series of sentences which the student listens to. The student must discriminate between long and short utterances, "long" representing the unreduced form of a word or phrase and "short" the reduced form of a word or phrase. Each lesson ends with an exercise in which students demonstrate recognition of reduced utterances. The sentences in these exercises are all spoken on the tape in the reduced forms. The student writes in the proper English spelling in the blank spaces to show that he has recognized the reductions.

In Part One the reduced forms, which are represented in italics, employ the following phonetic symbols:

e = the sound in h*e*
ih = the sound in h*i*t
ay = the sound in l*a*te
a = the sound in th*a*t
ah = the sound in n*o*t
o = the sound in n*o*
u = the sound in c*ou*ld
er = the sound in h*er*
uh = the sound in b*u*t and *a*bout
i = the sound in l*i*ke
õ = the nasalized sound of o in d*o*n't
- = syllable separation
( ) = optional phoneme or softening of a phoneme
' = common contraction or dropped consonant

Part Two contains a series of dialogs which contain blanks. The student is to listen to each dialog on the tape and write in that part of the dialog which is not included in his text. The language of the dialogs contains reductions which have been presented in Part One. Each dialog has been developed around a "real world" situation. After the student has listened to a dialog or series of dialogs, the teacher may want the student to repeat the dialogs or to learn parts of them. At this point, the degree of emphasis to be placed on the correct reproduction of reduced utterances is left to the teacher.

For the benefit of the student and the teacher, Part Three contains activation exercises which have been based on the situations created in the dialogs. These exercises have been designed to allow the student to use the language. Thus, they are best used in conjunction with the dialogs as the dialogs are being used. The activation exercises are not designed to ask questions on the dialogs per se. It is hoped that the student will be able to apply what he has learned from the dialogs in actual communication. The teacher may want to use the activation exercises to stimulate further dialogs (or controlled conversations) on the theme of a dialog section in the text. The activation exercises can also be used as writing assignments in which students construct dialogs around the specific activation tasks.

It is hoped that by using this text the ESL student will become more aware of the features that occur naturally and commonly in the speech of native Americans.

Table of Contents

PART ONE

PRESENTATION
□ LESSONS

Presentation Lessons

Lesson One: Reduced Forms of <u>And</u> and <u>Or</u>

Part A: <u>And</u>

Listen to the following reductions. Repeat the short version.

Long: John and I   Short: John and I
                                                              John -n- I

Long: coffee and tea   Short: coffee and tea
                                                              coffee -n- tea

Long: salt and pepper   Short: salt and pepper
                                                              salt -n- pepper

Long: Bill and Mary   Short: Bill and Mary
                                                              Bill -n- Mary

Long: French fries and a coke   Short: French fries and a coke
                                                              French fries -n- a coke

Long: come and see   Short: come and see
                                                              come -n- see

Long: boys and girls   Short: boys and girls
                                                              boys -n- girls

**Exercise A: Listen to the following sentences. If you hear the long version, circle LONG.
If you hear the short version, circle SHORT.**

1.	He and I are leaving now.	LONG	SHORT
2.	The students and the teacher are taking a break.	LONG	SHORT
3.	Please pass me the salt and pepper.	LONG	SHORT
4.	Sit down and fill out this form.	LONG	SHORT
5.	There is a radio and a stereo in the living room.	LONG	SHORT

Lesson One: (Continued)

Part B: <u>Or</u>

Listen to the following reductions. Repeat the short version.

Long: Bill or Gill   Short: Bill or Gill
                                                      Bill-er Gill

Long: this morning or this afternoon   Short: this morning or this afternoon
                                                      this morning-er this afternoon

Long: dinner or drinks   Short: dinner or drinks
                                                      dinner-er drinks

Long: a hamburger or a cheeseburger   Short: a hamburger or a cheeseburger
                                                      a hamburger-er a cheeseburger

Long: to go or to eat here   Short: to go or to eat here
                                                      to go-er to eat here

Long: now or later   Short: now or later
                                                      now-er later

Long: this way or that way   Short: this way or that way
                                                      this way-er that way

Exercise A: Listen to the following sentences. If you hear the long version, circle LONG. If you hear the short version, circle SHORT.

1. John or Bill will help you in a moment.   LONG   SHORT
2. Do you want coffee or tea?   LONG   SHORT
3. Was the exam easy or hard?   LONG   SHORT
4. There will be a holiday next Tuesday or   LONG   SHORT
    Wednesday.
5. Did you go to a movie or a play?   LONG   SHORT

Lesson One: (Continued)

Part C: **And** Contrasted With **Or**

Listen to the following contrasts. Repeat each phrase.

Contrast: a pen and a pencil   a pen or a pencil
a pen -n- a pencil   *a pen-er a pencil*

Contrast: John and I   John or I
John -n- I   *John-er I*

Contrast: salt and pepper   salt or pepper
salt -n- pepper   *salt-er pepper*

Contrast: work and study   work or study
work -n- study   *work-er study*

Contrast: a letter and a package   a letter or a package
a letter -n- a package   *a letter-er a package*

Contrast: radio and television   radio or television
radio -n- television   *radio-er television*

Exercise A: Fill in the blanks as you listen to the tape.

1. Do you want a hamburger _____ French fries?
2. Is the meeting on Tuesday _____ Wednesday?
3. Why don't you come up _____ see me sometime?
4. Please get me coffee _____ tea.
5. Was the test easy _____ difficult?
6. Have you seen John _____ Mary?
7. Come over about two _____ three o'clock.
8. The postman left a letter _____ a package for you.
9. Do you need a stamp _____ an envelope?
10. I will take a train _____ a bus to Baltimore.

Lesson Two: Contrast Between <u>A</u> and <u>The</u>

Listen to the following contrasts:

Contrast:	I do not have a pen.	I do not have the pen.
Contrast:	Do you have a key?	Do you have the key?
Contrast:	He works in a factory.	He works in the factory.
Contrast:	She broke a window.	She broke the window.

Exercise A: Listen to each of the following sentences and questions and repeat them.

1. It is in a book.   It is in the book.
2. Give this note to a teacher.   Give this note to the teacher.
3. He is standing next to a car.   He is standing next to the car.
4. I live near a bank.   I live near the bank.
5. I need a glass.   I need the glass.
6. Let's go to a movie.   Let's go to the movie.
7. Will you give Bill a message?   Will you give Bill the message?
8. Did you order a steak?   Did you order the steak?
9. Did you stay in a hotel?   Did you stay in the hotel?
10. John bought a desk.   John bought the desk.

Exercise B: Fill in the blanks as you listen to the tape. Some of the sentences contain no article.

1. I need _____ book.
2. Give it to _____ teacher.
3. Do you have _____ time?
4. She plays _____ piano.
5. It is in _____ box.
6. Would you like _____ coffee?
7. We had _____ flat tire.
8. I need _____ tune up for my car.
9. He wants _____ superburger.
10. The car rents for $10.00 _____ day.

11. Please send _____ taxi to my hotel.
12. I have to buy _____ loaf of bread.
13. I would like _____ beer.
14. Give him _____ money.
15. I will be there in _____ moment.
16. We will give you _____ call.
17. Keep _____ change.
18. Don works for _____ money.
19. Did you pay _____ rent?
20. Where is _____ frozen food section?

Lesson Three: Reduced Forms of Prepositions: <u>To</u>/<u>For</u>/<u>Of</u>

Part A: <u>To</u>

Listen to the following reductions. Repeat the short version.

Long: I used to live in Virginia.   Short: I used to live in Virginia.
                                                 I use-tuh live in Virginia.

Long: I would like to open an account.   Short: I would like to open an account.
                                                 I would like tuh-open an account.

Long: He wants to leave now.   Short: He wants to leave now.
                                                 He wants tuh leave now.

Long: We ought to go.   Short: We ought to go.
                                                 We ought tuh go.

Long: They hope to travel next year.   Short: They hope to travel next year.
                                                 They hope tuh travel next year.

Long: I gave the letter to Bob.   Short: I gave the letter to Bob.
                                                 I gave the letter tuh Bob.

Long: I am going to the post office.   Short: I am going to the post office.
                                                 I am going tuh the post office.

Long: I live next to a shopping center. Short: I live next to a shopping center.
                                                 I live next tuh-a shopping center.

Exercise A: Listen to the following sentences. If you hear the long version, circle LONG. If you hear the short version, circle SHORT.

1.	We plan to be home tonight.	LONG	SHORT
2.	He used to live on Maple Street.	LONG	SHORT
3.	They expect to arrive at 7:30 p.m.	LONG	SHORT
4.	I will not have time to finish this.	LONG	SHORT
5.	Will you talk to Bill this afternoon?	LONG	SHORT

Exercise B: Fill in the blanks as you listen to the tape.

1. They _____ live near me.
2. Bill _____ find a job this summer.
3. She _____ enter the university this fall.
4. Please give the message _____ .
5. I _____ go _____ tomorrow night.
6. She _____ study tonight.
7. I _____ make a long distance call.
8. They _____ the cafeteria.
9. Do you have time _____ me?
10. I mailed the package _____

Lesson Three: (Continued)

Part B: <u>For</u>

Listen to the following reductions. Repeat the short version.

Long: I have a letter for you.
Short: I have a letter for you.
I have a letter fe(r) you.

Long: They went to the store for bread.
Short: They went to the store for bread.
They went to the store fe(r) bread.

Long: I am looking for my English book.
Short: I am looking for my English book.
I am looking fe(r) my English book.

Long: This apartment is not for rent.
Short: This apartment is not for rent.
This apartment is not fe(r) rent.

Long: Thanks for calling.
Short: Thanks for calling.
Thanks fe(r) calling.

Exercise A: **Listen to the following sentences. If you hear the long version, circle LONG. If you hear the short version, circle SHORT.**

1. I have received a letter for you.   LONG   SHORT
2. We made reservations for dinner at 8:00.   LONG   SHORT
3. My friends are waiting for me.   LONG   SHORT
4. I went to Mexico for a vacation.   LONG   SHORT
5. Did you buy a present for Mary?   LONG   SHORT

Exercise B: **Fill in the blanks as you listen to the tape.**

1. Is there any mail _____ ?
2. The telegram is _____ .
3. They went home _____ .
4. I am looking _____ to read.
5. I think I will lie down _____ .

6. Do you have a message _____ ?
7. He has gone to lunch _____ .
8. This tie sells _____ .
9. Will you be away _____ ?
10. They're waiting _____ .

Lesson Three: (Continued)

Part C: <u>Of</u>

Listen to the following reductions. Repeat the short version.

Long: Some of the students are absent.

Short: Some of the students are absent.
Some-uh the students are absent.

Long: He is a friend of mine.

Short: He is a friend of mine.
He is a friend-uh mine.

Long: One of the windows is broken.

Short: One of the windows is broken.
One-uh the windows is broken.

Long: We have plenty of time.

Short: We have plenty of time.
We have plenty-uh time.

Long: I like both of them.

Short: I like both of them.
I like both-uh them.

Long: There is a lot of traffic today.

Short: There is a lot of traffic today.
There is a lot-uh traffic today.

Long: What is the meaning of this word?

Short: What is the meaning of this word?
What is the meaning-uh this word?

**Exercise A: Listen to the following sentences. If you hear the long version, circle LONG.
If you hear the short version, circle SHORT.**

1.	Please fill out one of these cards.	LONG	SHORT
2.	We do not have a lot of time to spare.	LONG	SHORT
3.	Take care of this matter for me.	LONG	SHORT
4.	They are standing in the back of the room.	LONG	SHORT
5.	She is a good friend of mine.	LONG	SHORT

Exercise B: Fill in the blanks as you listen to the tape.

1. Are they friends _____ ?

2. What's the coldest month _____ ?

3. Most _____ he is in his office.

4. Many _____ answers are wrong.

5. Two _____ are missing.

6. Give me some _____ .

7. I only have a couple _____ .

8. You made a lot _____ .

9. He is in front _____ .

10. This machine is _____ .

Lesson Four: Contractions With <u>Be</u>: Pronouns

Listen to the following contrasts. Repeat each sentence.

Contrast: I am right.   I'm right.
Contrast: You are wrong.   You're wrong.
Contrast: He is over there.   He's over there.
Contrast: She is my sister.   She's my sister.
Contrast: It is really cold today.   It's really cold today.
Contrast: We are sorry.   We're sorry.
Contrast: They are standing outside.   They're standing outside.

Exercise A: Fill in the blanks as you listen to the tape.

1. _____ trying to get in touch with Mr. Jackson.

2. _____ waiting for you in front of the building.

3. _____ leaving town for a couple of days.

4. _____ studying to be a dentist.

5. _____ late for the conference this morning.

6. _____ $14.00 for a single room.

7. _____ thinking about taking a trip to California.

8. _____ the best doctor in the city.

9. _____ friends of mine.

10. _____ almost time for the movie to begin.

Lesson Five: Contractions With <u>Be</u>:
Nouns/Question Words/<u>Here</u>/<u>There</u>/<u>That</u>

Listen to the following contrasts. Repeat each sentence.

Contrast:	Bob is my brother.	Bob's my brother.
Contrast:	What is this?	What's this?
Contrast:	Where is Helen?	Where's Helen?
Contrast:	Who is your boss?	Who's your boss?
Contrast:	Here is my passport.	Here's my passport.
Contrast:	There is your key.	There's your key.
Contrast:	That is a mistake.	That's a mistake.
Contrast:	The room is empty.	The room's empty.

Exercise A: Fill in the blanks as you listen to the tape.

1. _____ at the front door?
2. _____ a lot of work to do.
3. _____ reserving us a table at the restaurant.
4. _____ the sale price of this blouse?
5. _____ the flight number?
6. _____ your key.
7. _____ ready for your signature.
8. _____ the bus terminal from here?
9. _____ considering changing his present job.
10. _____ a restaurant in the lobby of the hotel.

Lesson Six: Contractions With <u>Will</u>

Listen to the following contrasts. Repeat each sentence.

Contrast:	I will be ready in a minute.	I'll be ready in a minute.
Contrast:	You will pass the exam.	You'll pass the exam.
Contrast:	He will help you.	He'll help you.
Contrast:	She will arrive soon.	She'll arrive soon.
Contrast:	It will rain later.	It'll rain later.
Contrast:	We will do it.	We'll do it.
Contrast:	They will be here.	They'll be here.
Contrast:	There will be enough.	There'll be enough.
Contrast:	That will do for now.	That'll do for now.
Contrast:	Mike will send for his things.	Mike'll send for his things.

Exercise A: Fill in the blanks as you listen to the tape.

1. _____ be a deposit of $10.00 to hold your tickets for you.
2. _____ try to do the shopping before I come home this evening.
3. _____ be much cooler tomorrow.
4. _____ know the answer, I'm sure.
5. _____ probably pay for the groceries with a check.
6. _____ be a short intermission after the first act.
7. _____ find the book on the reserve shelf in the library.
8. _____ call me back in a few minutes.
9. _____ be away all weekend.
10. _____ exam you now.

Lesson Seven: Contractions With <u>Have</u>/<u>Has</u> in the Present Perfect

Listen to the following contrasts. Repeat each sentence.

Contrast:	I have been here before.	I've been here before.
Contrast:	You have seen them.	You've seen them.
Contrast:	He has left.	He's left.
Contrast:	She has gone.	She's gone.
Contrast:	It has rained.	It's rained.
Contrast:	We have done it.	We've done it.
Contrast:	They have returned.	They've returned.
Contrast:	Bill has arrived.	Bill's arrived.
Contrast:	There has been an accident.	There's been an accident.
Contrast:	That has happened before.	That's happened before.

Exercise A: Fill in the blanks as you listen to the tape.

1. _____ seen this movie before.
2. _____ already left.
3. _____ been here for a long time.
4. _____ gone to school by now.
5. _____ spent all our money.
6. _____ been going on for a long time.
7. _____ been elected president of the engineering club.
8. _____ taught English for many years.
9. _____ tried to call you all morning.
10. _____ made a reservation for you at the Camelback Inn.

Lesson Eight: Contractions With <u>Would</u>

Listen to the following contrasts. Repeat each sentence.

Contrast:	I would like some tea.	I'd like some tea.
Contrast:	You would enjoy this.	You'd enjoy this.
Contrast:	He would like to come.	He'd like to come.
Contrast:	She would like an appointment.	She'd like an appointment.
Contrast:	We would like to talk to you.	We'd like to talk to you.
Contrast:	They would like to leave.	They'd like to leave.
Contrast:	Bob would prefer to finish this.	Bob'd prefer to finish this.
Contrast:	It would be better to eat now.	It'd be better to eat now.
Contrast:	There would be a lot of food.	There'd be a lot of food.

Exercise A: Fill in the blanks as you listen to the tape.

1. _____ dessert now, please.
2. _____ to open a savings account and a checking account.
3. _____ to ask you a few questions if you have time.
4. _____ glad to have you stay with us.
5. _____ to work for a long time to raise the money.
6. _____ you a coke, but there's not one in the house.
7. _____ nice to get tickets to the ball game.
8. _____ answer to my question.
9. _____ that gift.
10. I think _____ that movie.

Lesson Nine: Contractions With <u>Had</u>: Past Perfect/<u>Had</u> <u>Better</u>

Listen to the following contrasts. Repeat each sentence.

Contrast:	They had finished dinner at 8:00.	They'd finished dinner at 8:00.
Contrast:	She had already seen the movie.	She'd already seen the movie.
Contrast:	We had left by midnight.	We'd left by midnight.
Contrast:	I had better do this now.	I'd better do this now.
Contrast:	You had better go now.	You'd better go now.
Contrast:	He had better write it down.	He'd better write it down.

Exercise A: Fill in the blanks as you listen to the tape.

1.   I think _____ go now.
2.   _____ finish this book this week.
3.   _____ write my family a letter.
4.   _____ that film, but we saw it again.
5.   _____ listen to my advice.
6.   _____ home when you arrived.
7.   The doctor said that _____ .
8.   _____ a plumber.
9.   _____ ahead for hotel reservations.
10.   John went back to the office because _____ his glasses.

Lesson Ten: Contractions With <u>Not</u>

Listen to the following contrasts. Repeat each sentence.

Contrast: It is not time to leave.   It isn't time to leave.
Contrast: There are not any classes today. There aren't any classes today.
Contrast: I was not able to call you.   I wasn't able to call you.
Contrast: They were not here last week.   They weren't here last week.
Contrast: I have not seen him.   I haven't seen him.
Contrast: He has not arrived yet.   He hasn't arrived yet.
Contrast: Jim had not arrived at 7:00.   Jim hadn't arrived at 7:00.
Contrast: They would not go with us.   They wouldn't go with us.
Contrast: You should not be so careless.   You shouldn't be so careless.
Contrast: We could not hear the speaker.   We couldn't hear the speaker.
Contrast: You cannot do that.   You can't do that.
Contrast: They will not listen to us.   They won't listen to us.
Contrast: They do not want to come.   They don't want to come.
Contrast: He does not speak any English.   He doesn't speak any English.
Contrast: He did not say that.   He didn't say that.

Exercise A: Fill in the blanks as you listen to the tape.

1. He _____ in school last year.
2. They _____ come back yet.
3. This _____ the right telephone number.
4. There _____ many people here today.
5. You _____ work so hard.
6. She _____ found her key.
7. I _____ call you last night.
8. We _____ understand the professor.
9. The child _____ eat.
10. I _____ be able to see you tonight.
11. He said he _____ been there.
12. They _____ happy in the apartment.
13. There _____ enough seats.
14. That _____ make sense.
15. I _____ speak English very well.
16. They _____ like what he said.
17. He _____ work here any more.
18. We _____ interested in that.
19. She _____ help me with my problem.
20. You _____ be so careless.

Lesson Eleven: Contrast Between <u>Isn't</u> and <u>Wasn't</u>

Listen to the following contrasts. Repeat each sentence.

Contrast:	He isn't a student.	He wasn't a student.
Contrast:	She isn't late.	She wasn't late.
Contrast:	It isn't raining.	It wasn't raining.
Contrast:	The child isn't listening.	The child wasn't listening.
Contrast:	The price isn't high.	The price wasn't high.
Contrast:	The girl isn't at home.	The girl wasn't at home.
Contrast:	The number isn't listed.	The number wasn't listed.
Contrast:	The problem isn't serious.	The problem wasn't serious.

Exercise A: Fill in the blanks as you listen to the tape.

1. There _____ a service charge for the installation.
2. It _____ time to leave.
3. There _____ a message for you at the front desk.
4. The food _____ ready.
5. The football game _____ over until 10:30.
6. There _____ a chance of getting there on time.
7. This dress _____ properly marked.
8. Mr. Jackson _____ checking out of the hotel until later.
9. The immigration office _____ open on Monday.
10. Flight 782 _____ due until 12:30 p.m.

Lesson Twelve: Contrast Between <u>Aren't</u> and <u>Weren't</u>

Listen to the following contrasts. Repeat each sentence.

Contrast:	They aren't interested in leaving.	They weren't interested in leaving.
Contrast:	The apartments aren't furnished.	The apartments weren't furnished.
Contrast:	The utilities aren't included.	The utilities weren't included.
Contrast:	The elevators aren't working.	The elevators weren't working.
Contrast:	The department stores aren't open.	The department stores weren't open.
Contrast:	There aren't many people in line.	There weren't many people in line.
Contrast:	The school fees aren't too high.	The school fees weren't too high.
Contrast:	The Bensons aren't at home.	The Bensons weren't at home.

Exercise A: Fill in the blanks as you listen to the tape.

1. There _____ many things left to do.
2. The workers _____ happy with their contract.
3. The repairmen _____ coming until later.
4. They _____ having any problems.
5. Jack and Bill _____ at work.
6. There _____ many tickets left for the play.
7. The withdrawal slips _____ on the counter.
8. The banks _____ open on the weekend.
9. The forms _____ filled out correctly.
10. There _____ any vacancies at the motel.

Lesson Thirteen: Reduced Forms of Words Beginning with Aspirated "H"

Listen to the following reductions. Repeat the short version.

Long: I'll call her again tonight.

Short: I'll call her again tonight.
I'll call 'er again tonight.

Long: I gave him your message.

Short: I gave him your message.
I gave 'im your message.

Long: I think he's waiting to see you.

Short: I think he's waiting to see you.
I think 'e's waiting to see you.

Long: Come here a minute.

Short: Come here a minute.
Come 'ere a minute.

Long: Did Joe find his book?

Short: Did Joe find his book?
Did Joe find 'is book?

Exercise A: Listen to the following sentences. If you hear the long version, circle LONG. If you hear the short version, circle SHORT.

1. Give it to him.   LONG   SHORT
2. It's her application.   LONG   SHORT
3. Come here, please.   LONG   SHORT
4. Dan lost his book.   LONG   SHORT
5. I think he's in the cafeteria.   LONG   SHORT

Exercise B: Fill in the blanks as you listen to the tape.

1. Waiter, come _____ a minute.
2. Is that _____ brother?
3. Do you know _____ well?
4. Is this _____ seat?
5. Give _____ _____ ticket.
6. He hasn't been _____ all day.
7. Did you see _____ at the bank?
8. I think this is _____ check.
9. Are you going to speak to _____ later this week?
10. I need to buy a gift for _____ .

Lesson Fourteen: Contrast Between Reduced Forms of Them/Him

Part A: Them

Listen to the following reductions. Repeat the short version.

Long: I saw them yesterday.

Short: I saw them yesterday.
I saw 'em yesterday.

Long: I'll give them your message.

Short: I'll give them your message.
I'll give 'em your message.

Long: I told them you would call back.

Short: I told them you would call back.
I told 'em you would call back.

Long: Do you know them?

Short: Do you know them?
Do you know 'em?

Long: Have you ever met them before?

Short: Have you ever met them before?
Have you ever met 'em before?

Part B: Them/Him

Listen to the following contrasts. Repeat each sentence.

Contrast: I saw them yesterday.
I saw 'em yesterday.

I saw him yesterday.
I saw 'im yesterday.

Contrast: I told them to leave.
I told 'em to leave.

I told him to leave.
I told 'im to leave.

Contrast: Have them call me.
Have 'em call me.

Have him call me.
Have 'im call me.

Exercise A: Fill in the blanks as you listen to the tape.

1. Let me look at _____ again.
2. I'll put _____ behind the cash register.
3. Let _____ do the work.
4. Tell _____ Joe sent you.
5. Did you ask _____ if we could have the day off?
6. Have _____ call _____ .
7. I'll take three _____ .
8. Why don't you write _____ a letter?
9. Both _____ are out of order.
10. One _____ is more expensive than the other.

Lesson Fifteen: Reduced Forms of Verb-ing

Listen to the following reductions. Repeat the short version.

Long: I'm going home.   Short: I'm going home.
                                                       I'm go-in home.

Long: Where are you going?   Short: Where are you going?
                                                       Where are you go-in?

Long: He's working overseas.   Short: He's working overseas.
                                                       He's work-in overseas.

Long: What are you doing?   Short: What are you doing?
                                                       What are you do-in?

Long: Is the car being repaired?   Short: Is the car being repaired?
                                                       Is the car be-in repaired?

Long: Are you calling about the ad?   Short: Are you calling about the ad?
                                                       Are you call-in about the ad?

Long: They aren't leaving until Monday.   Short: They aren't leaving until Monday.
                                                       They aren't leav-in until Monday.

Exercise A: Listen to the following sentences. If you hear the long version, circle LONG. If you hear the short version, circle SHORT.

1.	Where are you going tonight?	LONG	SHORT
2.	I'm looking for a blouse, size 10.	LONG	SHORT
3.	Are you expecting him soon?	LONG	SHORT
4.	What are you doing later on?	LONG	SHORT
5.	I'm learning to speak English.	LONG	SHORT

Exercise B: Fill in the blanks as you listen to the tape.

1.   He _____ to Los Angeles next week.
2.   Who _____ with you now?
3.   He _____ some money from the bank.
4.   I _____ to learn English.
5.   He _____ the newspaper.
6.   We _____ thrown out of our apartment.
7.   She _____ to find a place to live.
8.   How _____ today?
9.   They're _____ fired.
10. I _____ here for three years.

Lesson Sixteen: Reduced Forms of Going To/Want To/ Have To

Listen to the following reductions. Repeat the short version.

Long: I'm going to leave now.

Long: Are you going to stay here?

Long: I want to go with you.

Long: Do you want to come with us?

Long: I'll have to write a check.

Long: Do you have to leave now?

Short: I'm going to leave now.
I'm guh-nuh leave now.

Short: Are you going to stay here?
Are you guh-nuh stay here?

Short: I want to go with you.
I wuh-nuh go with you.

Short: Do you want to come with us?
Do you wuh-nuh come with us?

Short: I'll have to write a check.
I'll haf-tuh write a check.

Short: Do you have to leave now?
Do you haf-tuh leave now?

Exercise A: Listen to the following sentences. If you hear the long version, circle LONG. If you hear the short version, circle SHORT.

1.	I'm going to leave now.	LONG	SHORT
2.	Do you want to come with us?	LONG	SHORT
3.	We have to call a taxi.	LONG	SHORT
4.	I don't want to take a taxi.	LONG	SHORT
5.	They're going to call a cab.	LONG	SHORT

Exercise B: Fill in the blanks as you listen to the tape.

1. We _____ leave at 9:00.
2. They _____ move to Los Angeles.
3. Do you _____ go home now?
4. _____ be your new roomate?
5. _____ hand in that assignment?
6. _____ her sometime?
7. _____ it by April 15.
8. _____ be fired for his mistake.
9. _____ bother us anymore.
10. _____ buy him a gift.

Lesson Seventeen: Reduced Forms of <u>Be</u> in Questions (Present Tense)

Listen to the following reductions. Repeat the short version.

Long: Are you ready to go?

Short: Are you ready to go?
Ah(r)-yuh ready to go?

Long: Am I late?

Short: Am I late?
Mi late?

Long: Is he a friend of yours?

Short: Is he a friend of yours?
Ze a friend of yours?

Long: Is she the new director?

Short: Is she the **new** director?
Ih-she the new director?

Long: Is it serious?

Short: Is it serious?
Zit serious?

Long: Are we going anywhere tonight?

Short: Are we going anywhere tonight?
Ah(r)-we going anywhere tonight?

Long: Are they leaving now?

Short: Are they leaving now?
Ah(r)-they leaving now?

Long: Is there any food left?

Short: Is there any food left?
Z-(th)ere any food left?

Long: Is this the right place?

Short: Is this the right place?
Z-(th)is the right place?

Long: Are these seats taken?

Short: Are these seats taken?
Ah(r)-these seats taken?

Exercise A: Listen to the following sentences. If you hear the long version, circle LONG. If you hear the short version, circle SHORT.

1. Is she studying English?	LONG	SHORT
2. Are we having class next Friday?	LONG	SHORT
3. Is there any tea left?	LONG	SHORT
4. Is he a friend of yours?	LONG	SHORT
5. Is it OK if I smoke?	LONG	SHORT
6. Is this the right bus?	LONG	SHORT
7. Are you doing anything tonight?	LONG	SHORT
8. Am I late?	LONG	SHORT
9. Is that your car?	LONG	SHORT
10. Are you new in town?	LONG	SHORT

Exercise B: Fill in the blanks as you listen to the tape.

1. _____ in this class or the other one?
2. _____ what you mean?
3. _____ staying at this hotel?
4. _____ cold outside today?
5. _____ the correct application form?
6. _____ any food left?
7. _____ all right if I smoke?
8. _____ out of town?
9. _____ making too much noise?
10. _____ finished with the lesson?

Lesson Eighteen: Reduced Forms of <u>Be</u> in Questions (Past Tense)

Listen to the following reductions. Repeat the short version.

Long: Was I supposed to be there?

Short: Was I supposed to be there?
Wuh-zi supposed to be there?

Long: Was she on time?

Short: Was she on time?
Wuh-she on time?

Long: Was he with you last night?

Short: Was he with you last night?
Wuh-ze with you last night?

Long: Was it raining this morning?

Short: Was it raining this morning?
Wuh-zit raining this morning?

Long: Were you in class yesterday?

Short: Were you in class yesterday?
We(r)-yuh in class yesterday?

Long: Were we blamed for that?

Short: Were we blamed for that?
We(r)-we blamed for that?

Long: Were they talking about me?

Short: Were they talking about me?
We(r)-they talking about me?

Long: Was this your seat?

Short: Was this your seat?
Wuh-z-(th)is your seat?

Exercise A: Listen to the following sentences. If you hear the long version, circle LONG. If you hear the short version, circle SHORT.

1.	Was she trying to telephone us?	LONG	SHORT
2.	Were you in the U.S. last year?	LONG	SHORT
3.	Were we invited to the party?	LONG	SHORT
4.	Were there any problems with it?	LONG	SHORT
5.	Was he at home last night?	LONG	SHORT

Exercise B: Fill in the blanks as you listen to the tape.

1. _____ your idea?
2. _____ another answer to the problem?
3. _____ speaking to me?
4. _____ supposed to show up for the meeting?
5. _____ able to go to the bank today?
6. _____ cold in Vancouver?
7. _____ your fiancé?
8. _____ chosen for the committee?
9. _____ gloves on sale?
10. _____ at school today?

Lesson Nineteen: Contrasts With <u>Be</u> in Questions (Present and Past Tense)

Listen to the following contrasts. Repeat each sentence.

Contrast: Are you a tourist?   Were you a tourist?
Ah(r)-yuh a tourist?   *We(r)-yuh a tourist?*

Contrast: Is he absent?   Was he absent?
Ze absent?   *Wuh-ze absent?*

Contrast: Is she in this class?   Was she in this class?
Ih-she in this class?   *Wuh-she in this class?*

Contrast: Is it cold outside?   Was it cold outside?
Zit cold outside?   *Wuh-zit cold outside?*

Contrast: Are we late?   Were we late?
Ah(r)-we late?   *We(r)-we late?*

Contrast: Are they talking about us?   Were they talking about us?
Ah(r)-they talking about us?   *We(r)-they talking about us?*

Contrast: Is there anything to drink?   Was there anything to drink?
Z-(th)ere anything to drink?   *Wuh-z-(th)ere anything to drink?*

Exercise A: Fill in the blanks as you listen to the tape.

1. A: _____ ready to go?
   B: No, wait a minute. I have something else to do.

2. A: _____ raining this morning?
   B: No, but it's raining now.

3. A: _____ taking an airplane to Boston?
   B: No, I think she's going by bus.

4. A: _____ anything else you need at the store?
   B: Why don't you pick up some milk?

5. A: _____ walking on University Avenue this morning?
   B: Oh, yes. I was on my way to the post office.

6. A: _____ absent today?
   B: Well, I guess so. I haven't seen him all day.

7. A: _____ your first visit to Dr. Jones?
   B: No, I was here once before.

8. A: _____ our assignment?
   B: Yes. Didn't you do it?

9. A: How do you like my new shoes?
   B: _____ expensive?

10. A: _____ seats taken?
    B: No, they aren't. Please sit down.

Lesson Nineteen: (Continued)

11. A: _____ any food left?
    B: No. It was all gone.

12. A: _____ your sister?
    B: No. She's my cousin.

13. A: _____ ever in Alaska?
    B: No. I've never been there.

14. A: _____ on time for the meeting?
    B: No. He was a few minutes late.

15. A: _____ Room 213?
    B: No. This is 212. 213 is across the hall.

Lesson Twenty: Reduced Forms of <u>Be</u> in Wh-Questions (Present Tense)

Listen to the following reductions. Repeat the short version.

Long: Where are you going?
Short: Where are you going?
Where-e(r)-yuh going?

Long: When is he in his office?
Short: When is he in his office?
When-ze in his office?

Long: What is she doing now?
Short: What is she doing now?
Wuh-dih-she doing now?

Long: Why are they leaving so soon?
Short: Why are they leaving so soon?
Why-e(r)-they leaving so soon?

Long: What am I supposed to do?
Short: What am I supposed to do?
Wuh-duh-mi supposed to do?

Long: When is it going to begin?
Short: When is it going to begin?
When-zit going to begin?

Long: When are we being transferred?
Short: When are we being transferred?
When-e(r)-we being transferred?

Exercise A: Listen to the following sentences. If you hear the long version, circle LONG. If you hear the short version, Circle SHORT.

1.	When are you going to New York?	LONG	SHORT
2.	Why are there so many people here?	LONG	SHORT
3.	How is this made?	LONG	SHORT
4.	What is it like in Las Vegas?	LONG	SHORT
5.	What is he doing in New York?	LONG	SHORT
6.	Why is she in such a hurry?	LONG	SHORT
7.	How are we going to pay the rent?	LONG	SHORT

Exercise B: Fill in the blanks as you listen to the tape.

1. _____ planning to do this evening?
2. _____ standing in line over there?
3. _____ supposed to do this assignment?
4. _____ to do tonight?
5. _____ arriving?
6. _____ going to be ready?
7. _____ be on television?
8. _____ taking us next weekend?
9. _____ going to find his house?
10. _____ doing on the table?
11. _____ located?
12. _____ talking about?
13. _____ going to get there?
14. _____ picking you up?
15. _____ meaning of this word?

Lesson Twenty-one: Reduced Forms of <u>Be</u> in Wh-Questions (Past Tense)

Listen to the following reductions. Repeat the short version.

Long: Why were you so late?

Short: Why were you so late?
Why-we(r)-yuh so late?

Long: Where was he yesterday?

Short: Where was he yesterday?
Where-wuh-ze yesterday?

Long: What was she doing last night?

Short: What was she doing last night?
Wuh(t)-wuh-she doing last night?

Long: Who were they talking to?

Short: Who were they talking to?
Who-we(r)-they talking to?

Long: Where was it found?

Short: Where was it found?
Where-wuh-zit found?

Long: When was I supposed to be there?

Short: When was I supposed to be there?
When-wuh-zi supposed to be there?

Long: When were we told to do that?

Short: When were we told to do that?
When-we(r) we told to do that?

Exercise A: Listen to the following sentences. If you hear the long version, circle LONG. If you hear the short version, circle SHORT.

1.	Where were you in 1972?	LONG	SHORT
2.	How was he feeling yesterday?	LONG	SHORT
3.	Who was he talking to just now?	LONG	SHORT
4.	Why were they upset?	LONG	SHORT
5.	What were we supposed to do?	LONG	SHORT

Exercise B: Fill in the blanks as you listen to the tape.

1. _____ working for?
2. _____ so angry with us?
3. _____ planning to do?
4. _____ informed of the accident?
5. _____ supposed to meet Bill?
6. _____ standing in line yesterday?
7. _____ a student at UCLA?
8. _____ those gloves?
9. _____ yesterday?
10. _____ talking to this morning?
11. _____ supposed to go?
12. _____ supposed to do this?
13. _____ with last night?
14. _____ lost?
15. _____ ?

Lesson Twenty-two: Contrasts With <u>Be</u> in Wh-Questions (Present and Past Tense)

Listen to the following contrasts:

Contrast: Where are you living?
Where-e(r)-yuh living?

Where were you living?
Where-we(r)-yuh living?

Contrast: When is he in his office?
When-ze in his office?

When was he in his office?
When-wuh-ze in his office?

Contrast: How is she feeling?
How-ih-she feeling?

How was she feeling?
How-wuh-she feeling?

Contrast: What are we talking about?
Wuh(d)-e(r)-we talking about?

What were we talking about?
Wuh(t)-we(r)-we talking about?

Contrast: Why are they speaking so loudly?
Why-e(r)-they speaking so loudly?

Why were they speaking so loudly?
Why-we(r)-they speaking so loudly?

Contrast: When is it over?
When-zit over?

When was it over?
When-wuh-zit over?

Exercise A: Fill in the blanks as you listen to the tape.

1. A: _____ doing tonight?
   B: Nothing much. Do you have any suggestions?

2. A: _____ feeling?
   B: The doctor says he can go home tomorrow.

3. A: _____ going to stop raining?
   B: I don't know. I'm really sick of this bad weather.

4. A: _____ so late?
   B: I had a flat tire. That's why!

5. A: _____ talking about?
   B: Just the same old thing, as usual.

6. A: _____ standing in line?
   B: Don't you know? Tonight is the Charles Mingus concert.

7. A: _____ so upset?
   B: Don't ask me. I don't understand it either.

8. A: _____ calling on the phone?
   B: The dentist's office. She needs to make an appointment.

9. A: _____ in Europe?
   B: From 1969 to 1973.

10. A: _____ from here?
    B: It's not far. About three hours by car.

11. A: _____ plane arriving?
    B: It's due in from Denver at 9:00.

☐

12. A: _____ for a one-way ticket?
    B: $22.50 plus tax.

13. A: _____ in her office?
    B: She's usually there in the early afternoon.

14. A: _____ so loudly?
    B: I think she's hard of hearing.

15. A: _____ last night when I called?
    B: I was watching television.

Lesson Twenty-three: Reduced Forms of Don't/ Doesn't/Didn't in Statements

Listen to the following reductions. Repeat the short version.

Long: I don't like coffee.

Short: I don't like coffee.
I dõ(n) like coffee.

Long: They don't remember us.

Short: They don't remember us.
They dõ(n) remember us.

Long: He doesn't live here.

Short: He doesn't live here.
He duhz-n live here.

Long: It doesn't cost much.

Short: It doesn't cost much.
It duhz-n cost much.

Long: I didn't know that.

Short: I didn't know that.
I dih-n know that.

Long: She didn't tell me.

Short: She didn't tell me.
She dih-n tell me.

Exercise A: **Listen to the following sentences. If you hear the long version, circle LONG. If you hear the short version, circle SHORT.**

1. It doesn't take long to get there.   LONG   SHORT
2. They didn't do the assignment.   LONG   SHORT
3. We don't have enough time.   LONG   SHORT
4. He didn't know what to do.   LONG   SHORT
5. Joe doesn't live here anymore.   LONG   SHORT

Exercise B: **Fill in the blanks as you listen to the tape.**

1. You _____ need to worry about it.
2. He _____ remember anything I said.
3. My watch _____ work.
4. Mary _____ have any time to call you.
5. The meeting _____ start until twelve.
6. Two wrongs _____ make a right.
7. I _____ understand the question.
8. He _____ here anymore.
9. I _____ a reservation.
10. It _____ very much.

Lesson Twenty-four: Reduced Forms of <u>Do</u>/<u>Does</u> in Questions

Listen to the following reductions. Repeat the short version.

Long: Do you know her?   Short: Do you know her?
                                              D-yuh know her?

Long: Does he live here?   Short: Does he live here?
                                              (T)se live here?

Long: Does she have your number?   Short: Does she have your number?
                                              Duh-she have your number?

Long: Does it ever snow here?   Short: Does it ever snow here?
                                              (D)zit ever snow here?

Long: Does that include tax?   Short: Does that include tax?
                                              (D)z(th)at include tax?

Long: Do we need it?   Short: Do we need it?
                                              Duh-we need it?

Long: Do they work for you?   Short: Do they work for you?
                                              Duh-they work for you?

Exercise A: Listen to the following sentences. If you hear the long version, circle LONG. If you hear the short version, circle SHORT.

1. Do you speak English?   LONG   SHORT
2. Does it work like this?   LONG   SHORT
3. Does she know how to swim?   LONG   SHORT
4. Do they know the way to the office?   LONG   SHORT
5. Do we go this way or that way?   LONG   SHORT

Exercise B: Fill in the blanks as you listen to the tape.

1. _____ speak any English?
2. _____ really have to go now?
3. _____ read page 40 or 14?
4. _____ like coffee with cream and sugar in it?
5. _____ know how to get to our apartment?
6. _____ at 8:00 or 9:00?
7. _____ on the third floor?
8. _____ make any difference?
9. _____ downtown?
10. _____ play tennis?

Lesson Twenty-five: Reduced Forms of <u>Did</u> in Questions

Listen to the following reductions. Repeat the short version.

Long: Did you call in advance?

Short: Did you call in advance?
Juh call in advance?

Long: Did he pay back the money?

Short: Did he pay back the money?
De pay back the money?

Long: Did she call you last night?

Short: Did she call you last night?
Che call you last night?

Long: Did it rain last night?

Short: Did it rain last night?
Dit rain last night?

Long: Did that noise bother you?

Short: Did that noise bother you?
Dthat noise bother you?

Long: Did we win the football game?

Short: Did we win the football game?
Dih-we win the football game?

Long: Did they put in your phone?

Short: Did they put in your phone?
Dih-they put in your phone?

Exercise A: Listen to the following sentences. If you hear the long version, circle LONG. If you hear the short version, circle SHORT.

1.	Did he get the job?	LONG	SHORT
2.	Did you see the movie at the Paramount?	LONG	SHORT
3.	Did she remember your name?	LONG	SHORT
4.	Did they sign a lease on the apartment?	LONG	SHORT
5.	Did we have any homework?	LONG	SHORT

Exercise B: Fill in the blanks as you listen to the tape.

1. _____ send you a letter?
2. _____ call you last night?
3. _____ win the game?
4. _____ put in your phone?
5. _____ do the laundry?
6. _____ ever think of that?
7. _____ quit her job?
8. _____ to the meeting?
9. _____ on time?
10. _____ seem like a good thing to do?

Lesson Twenty-six: Contrast Between Reduced Forms of <u>Do</u>/<u>Does</u> and <u>Did</u> in Questions

Listen to the following contrasts. Repeat each sentence.

Contrast:	Do you live in New York? *D-yuh live in New York?*	Did you live in New York? *Juh live in New York?*
Contrast:	Does he know the answer? *(T)-se know the answer?*	Did he know the answer? *De know the answer?*
Contrast:	Does she visit you often? *Duh-she visit you often?*	Did she visit you often? *Che visit you often?*
Contrast:	Does it cost a lot? *(D)zit cost a lot?*	Did it cost a lot? *Dit cost a lot?*
Contrast:	Does that include tax? *(D)z(th)at include tax?*	Did that include tax? *Dthat include tax?*
Contrast:	Do we have any homework? *Duh-we have any homework?*	Did we have any homework? *Dih-we have any homework?*
Contrast:	Do they live near you? *Duh-they live near you?*	Did they live near you? *Dih-they live near you?*

Exercise A: Fill in the blanks as you listen to the tape.

1. _____ live here?
2. _____ have any money?
3. _____ speak English?
4. _____ ever rain in Arizona?
5. _____ have to go?
6. _____ work here?
7. _____ get the job?
8. _____ pay back the money?
9. _____ call you last night?
10. _____ win the basketball game?
11. _____ put in your phone?
12. _____ get the car repaired?
13. _____ go with you?
14. _____ live in Phoenix?
15. _____ have a room for rent?
16. _____ know the way?
17. _____ have any time to help us?
18. _____ know how to swim?
19. _____ buy our books here?
20. _____ accept checks?

Exercise B: Fill in the blanks as you listen to the tape.

1. A: _____ English at all?
   B: Oh, sure. I know a little English.

2. A: _____ in San Francisco?
   B: She used to, but she's in Seattle now.

3. A: _____ the money?
   B: No, not yet.

4. A: _____ to call the water department?
   B: Oh, no! I forgot.

Lesson Twenty-six: (Continued)

5. A: _____ with them?
   B: No, I went by myself.

6. A: _____ the question?
   B: Not completely. Can you repeat it?

7. A: _____ you often?
   B: About twice a week.

8. A: _____ have any butter?
   B: Un-unh, we'll have to buy some.

9. A: _____ cream in your coffee?
   B: Just a little bit.

10. A: _____ while you were in London?
    B: Just about every day.

Lesson Twenty-seven: Reduced Forms of Do/Does in Wh-Questions

Listen to the following reductions. Repeat the short version.

Long: Where do I have to go?

Short: Where do I have to go?
Where duh-wi have to go?

Long: What do you want for dinner?

Short: What do you want for dinner?
Wuh-duh-yuh want for dinner?

Long: Where does he live?

Short: Where does he live?
Where-ze live?

Long: Who does she work for?

Short: Who does she work for?
Who-duh-she work for?

Long: When does it start?

Short: When does it start?
When-zit start?

Long: How do we get there?

Short: How do we get there?
How-duh-we get there?

Long: What do they want?

Short: What do they want?
Wuh-duh-they want?

Long: Why does that cost so much?

Short: Why does that cost so much?
Why-z(th)at cost so much?

Exercise A: Listen to the following sentences. If you hear the long version, circle LONG. If you hear the short version, circle SHORT.

1.	When does it open?	LONG	SHORT
2.	What do you want to do?	LONG	SHORT
3.	Who does she work for?	LONG	SHORT
4.	How do you say that in Spanish?	LONG	SHORT
5.	What does he do for a living?	LONG	SHORT

Exercise B: Fill in the blanks as you listen to the tape.

1. _____ make a difference?
2. _____ keep the butter?
3. _____ take to get to Chicago from here?
4. _____ want your hair cut?
5. _____ do for a living?
6. _____ cost?
7. _____ your shopping?
8. _____ Houston?
9. _____ in the bag?
10. _____ to leave?

Lesson Twenty-eight: Reduced Forms of <u>Did</u> in Wh-Questions

Listen to the following reductions. Repeat the short version.

Long: Where did I put my keys?   Short: Where did I put my keys?
Where-di put my keys?

Long: What did you do last night?   Short: What did you do last night?
Wuh-juh do last night?

Long: When did he arrive?   Short: When did he arrive?
When-de arrive?

Long: Who did she give them to?   Short: Who did she give them to?
Who-che give them to?

Long: When did it start?   Short: When did it start?
When-dit start?

Long: Why did we have to leave?   Short: Why did we have to leave?
Why-d(ih)-we have to leave?

Long: What did they say to you?   Short: What did they say to you?
Wuh-d(ih)-they say to you?

Long: Where did that come from?   Short: Where did that come from?
Where-d(ih)-that come from?

Exercise A: Listen to the following sentences. If you hear the long version, circle LONG. If you hear the short version, circle SHORT.

1.	How much did that cost?	LONG	SHORT
2.	Where did she put the keys?	LONG	SHORT
3.	Why did you miss class?	LONG	SHORT
4.	Where did you buy that shirt?	LONG	SHORT
5.	When did they call you?	LONG	SHORT

Exercise B: Fill in the blanks as you listen to the tape.

1. _____ do last night?
2. _____ put the money?
3. _____ hear that?
4. _____ order for dinner?
5. _____ give it to?
6. _____ that story?
7. _____ that question?
8. _____ for dinner?
9. _____ that sweater?
10. _____ ?

Lesson Twenty-nine: Contrast Between Reduced Forms of <u>Do</u>/<u>Does</u> and <u>Did</u> in Wh-Questions

Listen to the following contrasts. Repeat each sentence.

Contrast: Where do I have to go?
Where-duh-wi have to go?

Where did I have to go?
Where-di have to go?

Contrast: What do you want for dinner?
Wuh-duh-yuh want for dinner?

What did you want for dinner?
Wuh-juh want for dinner?

Contrast: Where does he live?
Where-ze live?

Where did he live?
Where-de live?

Contrast: Who does she work for?
Who-duh-she work for?

Who did she work for?
Who-che work for?

Contrast: When does it start?
When-zit start?

When did it start?
When-dit start?

Contrast: Why do we have to leave?
Why-duh-we have to leave?

Why did we have to leave?
Why-d(ih)-we have to leave?

Contrast: What do they want?
Wuh-duh-they want?

What did they want?
Wuh-d(ih)-they want?

Contrast: What does that mean?
Wuht-s(th)at mean?

What did that mean?
Wuh-d(ih)-that mean?

Exercise A: Fill in the blanks as you listen to the tape.

1. _____ matter so much?
2. _____ want your steak cooked?
3. _____ hear that?
4. _____ arrive from Atlanta?
5. _____ order for dessert?
6. _____ cost to fix your car?
7. _____ buy that shirt?
8. _____ do when she found out?
9. _____ open for business?
10. _____ take to drive to Baltimore?
11. _____ pay the rent?
12. _____ think you can fix it?
13. _____ say that in Spanish?
14. _____ want to go?
15. _____ mean by that?
16. _____ matter so much to you?
17. _____ ever do that?
18. _____ know he'd get angry?
19. _____ work for?
20. _____ come from?

Exercise B: Fill in the blanks as you listen to the tape.

1. A: What a beautiful day. The sky's clear for a change.
   B: Yes, it is. _____ to clear up?

2. A: _____ your steak cooked?
   B: Medium rare, please.

3. A: _____ to see to clear up this error in my bill?
   B: You ought to contact Mrs. Robinson about that.

4. A: _____ the meeting?
   B: He had some urgent business to attend to.

5. A: _____ to him?
   B: She told him to come at 1:00.

Lesson Thirty: Reduced Forms of <u>Be</u> in Negative Questions

Listen to the following contrasts. Repeat each sentence.

Contrast: Aren't you a student?
Ah(r)n-chuh a student?

Weren't you a student?
We(r)n-chuh a student?

Contrast: Isn't she the director?
Ihz-n-she the director?

Wasn't she the director?
Wuhz-n-she the director?

Contrast: Isn't he a friend of yours?
Ihz-n-e a friend of yours?

Wasn't he a friend of yours?
Wuhz-n-e a friend of yours?

Contrast: Aren't we in the right seats?
Ah(r)n-(t)-we in the right seats?

Weren't we in the right seats?
We(r)n-(t)-we in the right seats?

Contrast: Isn't that expensive?
Ihz-n-(th)at expensive?

Wasn't that expensive?
Wuhz-n-(th)at expensive?

Contrast: Aren't there any seats left?
Ah(r)n-(t)-there any seats left?

Weren't there any seats left?
We(r)n-(t)-there any seats left?

Contrast: You're a student, aren't you?
You're a student, ah(r)n-chuh?

You were a student, weren't you?
You were a student, we(r)n-chuh?

Exercise A: Fill in the blanks as you listen to the tape.

1. _____ from Ohio?
2. _____ a beautiful day?
3. _____ a friend of yours, _____ ?
4. _____ your boss?
5. _____ at the meeting?
6. _____ any apartments for rent around here?
7. _____ a new student, _____ ?
8. _____ supposed to pay the rent today?
9. _____ going to refund your money?
10. _____ open yet?

Lesson Thirty-one:　Reduced Forms of <u>Do</u> in Negative Questions

Listen to the following reductions. Repeat each sentence.

Long:　Don't you want to go?	Short:　Don't you want to go? *Dõ(n)-chuh want to go?*
Long:　Don't they like it here?	Short:　Don't they like it here? *Dõ(n)-(t)they like it here?*
Long:　Doesn't he live here anymore?	Short:　Doesn't he live here anymore? *Duh-zuh-ne live here anymore?*
Long:　Doesn't she have a car?	Short:　Doesn't she have a car? *Duh-zuhn-she have a car?*
Long:　Doesn't it start at 9:00?	Short:　Doesn't it start at 9:00? *Duh-zuh-nit start at 9:00?*
Long:　Didn't you have a good time?	Short:　Didn't you have a good time? *Dih-n-chuh have a good time?*
Long:　Didn't they go with you?	Short:　Didn't they go with you? *Dih-n-(t) they go with you?*
Long:　Didn't she tell you the news?	Short:　Didn't she tell you the news? *Dih-n-she tell you the news?*
Long:　Didn't it rain last night?	Short:　Didn't it rain last night? *Dih-n-it rain last night?*
Long:　Didn't he call you?	Short:　Didn't he call you? *Dih-n-e call you?*

Exercise A:　Listen to the following questions. If you hear the long version, circle LONG. If you hear the short version, circle SHORT.

1.	Didn't she used to live in Miami, Florida?	LONG	SHORT
2.	Don't you think it's time to go?	LONG	SHORT
3.	Didn't it rain last night?	LONG	SHORT
4.	Don't you remember me?	LONG	SHORT
5.	Didn't he bring the beer with him?	LONG	SHORT

Exercise B:　Fill in the blanks as you listen to the tape.

1. _____ want to come along?

2. _____ see the movie last night?

3. _____ have any money?

4. _____ bring your camera?

5. _____ know how to swim?

6. _____ register at the desk?

Lesson Thirty-one: (Continued)

7.   _____ remind you of someone else?

8.   _____ want to see me today?

9.   _____ need to extend their visas?

10.   _____ have this dress in size 10?

11.   It rained last night, _____ ?

12.   She moved to the East, _____ ?

13.   You have some money, _____ ?

14.   Bill bought a house, _____ ?

15.   She used to work there, _____ ?

Lesson Thirty-two: Reduced Forms of <u>Has</u>/<u>Have</u> in Questions

Listen to the following reductions. Repeat the short version.

Long: Have you ever been to Arizona? | Short: Have you ever been to Arizona?
V-yuh ever been to Arizona?

Long: Have I ever lied to you? | Short: Have I ever lied to you?
Vi ever lied to you?

Long: Have they gone home already? | Short: Have they gone home already?
V-they gone home already?

Long: Have we forgotten anything? | Short: Have we forgotten anything?
V-we forgotten anything?

Long: Has he finished the report? | Short: Has he finished the report?
Ze finished the report?

Long: Has she started her new job? | Short: Has she started her new job?
Ha-she started her new job?

Long: Has it happened before? | Short: Has it happened before?
Zit happened before?

Long: Have there been any messages? | Short: Have there been any messages?
V-there been any messages?

Exercise A: Listen to the following questions. If you hear the long version, circle LONG. If you hear the short version, circle SHORT.

1. Has she started to work for I.B.M. yet?   LONG   SHORT
2. Have you called the plumber yet?   LONG   SHORT
3. Has he ever lied to you?   LONG   SHORT
4. Have they found an apartment?   LONG   SHORT
5. Have you tried to find it in the bookstore?   LONG   SHORT

Exercise B: Fill in the blanks as you listen to the tape.

1. _____ found a place to live?
2. _____ called her yet?
3. _____ ever been married?
4. _____ tried peanut butter?
5. _____ finished your assignment yet?
6. _____ the report?
7. _____ any messages for me?
8. _____ the problem?
9. _____ the news?
10. _____ yet?

Lesson Thirty-three: Reduced Forms of <u>Has</u>/<u>Have</u> in Statements

Listen to the following reductions. Repeat the short version.

Long: I have some work to do.

Long: You have a nice place.

Long: She has a good job.

Long: It has a lock on it.

Long: He has a lot of money.

Long: We have a lot to learn.

Long: They have a lot in common.

Short: I have some work to do.
I-av some work to do.

Short: You have a nice place.
Yuh-av a nice place.

Short: She has a good job.
She-as a good job.

Short: It has a lock on it.
It-as a lock on it.

Short: He has a lot of money.
He-as a lot of money.

Short: We have a lot to learn.
We-av a lot to learn.

Short: They have a lot in common.
They-av a lot in common.

Exercise A: **Listen to the following sentences. If you hear the long version, circle LONG. If you hear the short version, circle SHORT.**

1.	You have a good idea.	LONG	SHORT
2.	We have too many books.	LONG	SHORT
3.	He has your keys.	LONG	SHORT
4.	She has a ticket.	LONG	SHORT
5.	It has a good view.	LONG	SHORT

Exercise B: **Fill in the blanks as you listen to the tape.**

1. _____ more than we need.
2. _____ some free time this afternoon.
3. _____ a friend in the army.
4. _____ a new job.
5. _____ a new phone number.
6. _____ a headache.
7. _____ some good points and some bad points.
8. _____ an appointment for 2:30.
9. I think _____ change for a twenty.
10. _____ a savings account at this bank.

Lesson Thirty-four: Reduced Forms of Modals in Questions

Listen to the following reductions. Repeat the short version.

Long: Could he go with you?

Short: Could he go with you?
Cu-de go with you?

Long: Could you give me a ride?

Short: Could you give me a ride?
Cu-juh give me a ride?

Long: Would he like to come along?

Short: Would he like to come along?
Wu-de like to come along?

Long: Should you give this to her?

Short: Should you give this to her?
Shu-juh give this to her?

Long: Will you help me?

Short: Will you help me?
Wih(l)-yuh help me?

Long: Will she wait for us?

Short: Will she wait for us?
Wih(l)-she wait for us?

Long: Can you give me a hand?

Short: Can you give me a hand?
Ca-nyuh give me a hand?

Exercise A: Listen to the following questions. If you hear the long version, circle LONG. If you hear the short version, circle SHORT.

1.	Would you like a cup of coffee?	LONG	SHORT
2.	Can you lend me your key?	LONG	SHORT
3.	Could you open the window please?	LONG	SHORT
4.	Would he help us if we asked?	LONG	SHORT
5.	Will he be around this afternoon?	LONG	SHORT

Exercise B: Fill in the blanks as you listen to the tape.

1. _____ pick me up tomorrow?
2. _____ wait for me here?
3. _____ come along with you?
4. _____ stay with us tonight?
5. _____ really be true?
6. _____ be arrested for that?
7. _____ be helping you?
8. Where _____ something to eat?
9. When _____ over to see you?
10. What _____ with a million dollars?

Lesson Thirty-five: Reduced Forms with Modal Perfect in Statements

Listen to the following reductions. Repeat the short version.

Long: I should have gone with you.

Short: I should have gone with you.
I shu-duh(v) gone with you.

Long: He must have gone home already.

Short: He must have gone home already.
He must-stuh(v) gone home already.

Long: She could have helped you.

Short: She could have helped you.
She cu-duh(v) helped you.

Long: We would have come if you had asked us.

Short: We would have come if you had asked us.
We wu-duh(v) come if you had asked us.

Long: By 1981 he will have graduated.

Short: By 1981 he will have graduated.
By 1981 he wih-luh(v) graduated.

Long: He might have been there, but I didn't see him.

Short: He might have been there, but I didn't see him.
He mi-tuh(v) been there, but I didn't see him.

Long: You shouldn't have done that.

Short: You shouldn't have done that.
You shu-n-tuh(v) done that.

Exercise A: Listen to the following sentences. If you hear the long version, circle LONG. If you hear the short version, circle SHORT.

1. They could have left early, but I doubt it.   LONG   SHORT
2. We would have phoned, but there wasn't time.   LONG   SHORT
3. The stores will have closed by now.   LONG   SHORT
4. The plane might have been delayed.   LONG   SHORT
5. They really shouldn't have made that mistake.   LONG   SHORT

Exercise B: Fill in the blanks as you listen to the tape.

1. _____ said that.
2. _____ forgotten the conference.
3. _____ been mistaken.
4. _____ become a doctor, but he didn't.
5. _____ been the right answer.
6. _____ Robert knew so much about history.
7. The waiter _____ the orders.
8. The snow _____ by now.
9. _____ dinner if there had been enough time.
10. _____ lost.

51

Lesson Thirty-six: Deletion of Initial Verb Forms in Questions

Note: Sometimes in rapid conversation, initial verb forms are not only reduced, they are completely deleted from the question. This lesson offers exercise in recognizing the common patterns in which initial verb forms may be deleted. Deletions of this type are generally very informal.

Listen to the deletions which take place in the following questions.

Long: Do you want some tea?	Deleted: You want some tea?
Long: Do they know you?	Deleted: They know you?
Long: Did he call you last night?	Deleted: He call you last night?
Long: Did you buy that stereo yesterday?	Deleted: You buy that stereo yesterday?
Long: Have you seen him recently?	Deleted: You seen him recently?
Long: Has she been here?	Deleted: She been here?
Long. Is this your book?	Deleted: This your book?
Long: Are there any seats left?	Deleted: There any seats left?

Exercise A: Listen to the long and deleted version of each of the following questions. Repeat the deleted version of the question.

1. (Do) you have Bob's telephone number?
2. (Does) she know Glenda Jackson?
3. (Did) he find his notebook?
4. (Have) you ever been to El Paso?
5. (Has) he been in Tucson for long?
6. (Is) this Emily's math book?
7. (Are) there any cheap apartments in Tempe?
8. (Do) they arrive at 7:30 or 8:00?
9. (Did) you have much to do last weekend?
10. (Is) there any food in the refrigerator?

PART TWO

DIALOGS

Dialogs

1. Getting There

A. At the Airport

1. *Customer:* _____ flights ___ Las Vegas on Saturday?

   Agent: _____ flights at 9:30 a.m. ___ 3:40 p.m.

   Customer: _____ arrive in Las Vegas?

   Agent: 10:30 a.m. and 4:40 p.m.

   Customer: How much _____ fare?

   Agent: One way is $22.50 plus tax. Round trip is $38.75.

2. *Agent:* _____ fly: coach ___ first class?

   Customer: Coach is cheaper, _____ ?

   Agent: Yes, coach fare is more economical.

   Customer: I think ___ fly coach on the 9:30 a.m. flight.

3. *Agent:* Here you go, ma'am. _____ your boarding pass.

   Customer: _____ the departure gate?

   Agent: Gate 10. It's straight ahead past the security check area.

4. *Customer:* Which gate _____ my plane leave from?

   Agent: It leaves from Gate 22.

   Customer: _____ this way ___ that way?

   Agent: _____ your left. _____ hurry. _____ loading right now.

5. *Woman:* Excuse me. _____ five-thirty flight from Denver on time?

   Agent: No, ma'am. _____ delayed.

   Woman: Delayed? For how long?

   Agent: _____ at least an hour. _____ a bad snow storm in Denver.

B. Buses, Local and Long Distance

6. *Passenger:* Excuse me, driver. _____ bus go past _____ university?

   Driver: No, not this bus. _____ transfer downtown.

   Passenger: Which bus _____ take from there?

   Driver: I believe it's the number four bus.

7. Passenger: _____ bus take me ___ MacArthur Park?

   Driver: Nope. _____ transfer at Central Avenue.

   Passenger: Which bus _____ take?

   Driver: _____ Central Avenue buses go past ____ park.

8. Passenger: This bus goes past the university, _____ ?

   Driver: It goes near the university.

   Passenger: _____ get off?

   Driver: Get off at Fourth Street ____ walk two blocks east.

9. Passenger: This bus ____ take me to the Capitol Building, _____ ?

   Driver: Yep. It sure will.

   Passenger: How much is the fare?

   Driver: Fifty cents. Exact change.

   Passenger: Here you are.

   Driver: _____ it to me. Drop it _____ box.

10. Customer: How much _____ fare to San Francisco via Los Angeles?

    Agent: It's $55.

    Customer: _____ in L.A. _____ few days?

    Agent: Sure. Your ticket is good for three weeks.

11. Man: _____ bus stop ____ lunch?

    Woman: I think the driver said ____ stop at 12:30.

    Man: How long _____ eat?

    Woman: The lunch stop is for an hour.

C. Taxis

12. Man: Red Cab Taxi Company. _____ help you?

    Woman: Please send a taxi _____ Hilton Hotel.

    Man: _____ your name?

    Woman: Alice Jones.

    Man: A cab _____ there in ten minutes.

13. *Passenger:* _____ taxi taken?

    Driver: No. _____ ?

    Passenger: To the Lincoln Park Apartments. _____ on 44th Street.

    Driver: I know where they are. Get in.

14. *Driver:* Which terminal _____ ?

    Passenger: Japan Air Lines.

    Driver: Here you are, sir.

    Passenger: Fine. How much _____ fare?

    Driver: Six-forty.

    Passenger: _____ seven dollars. Keep ___ change.

D. Renting a Car

15. *Customer:* _____ possible ___ rent ___ car from here?

    Agent: Yes. _____ in advance?

    Customer: No, _____ . _____ just arrived in town.

    Agent: Well, all that we have available right now is a Nova.

    Customer: _____ be fine. How much _____ per day?

    Agent: Twenty dollars per day. There's no limit on mileage.

16. *Customer:* _____ rent a car _____ day.

    Agent: Fine, sir. _____ Pintos, Granadas, and Mercuries.

    Customer: Let's see. Which is the cheapest? The Pinto?

    Agent: That's right. _____ ten dollars a day, plus ten cents a mile.

17. *Agent:* How long _____ the car for?

    Customer: Three days at most.

    Agent: I _____ see your driver's license _____ major credit card.

    Customer: Here's my bank credit card. Will that do?

    Agent: That's fine.

E. Getting Directions

18.   *Woman:* _____ how _____ Paul's house from here?

        Man: Yeh. Stay on this road until you get __ Glenn Road. Then take __ left.

     Woman: Left on Glenn Road, OK . . . .

        Man: Stay on Glenn Road _____ about four blocks until you come __ Washington Street. Then turn right.

     Woman: Left on Glenn, right on Washington, ...

        Man: He lives at 222 Washington. _____ right side _____ street.

19.   *Man:* _____ turn right here?

     Woman: No. Keep going straight _____ turn _____ next light.

        Man: _____ at Scott Road?

     Woman: That's right. Turn right there.

20.   *Man:* _____ from here to L.A.?

     Woman: Oh, about seven hours by car.

        Man: _____ best way to get there?

     Woman: I-10 _____ fastest.

2. As Time Goes By

A. Making Appointments

21.   *Man:* _____ make an appointment to see Dr. Taylor.

 Receptionist: OK. Let's see. He's available on Tuesday _____ Thursday.

        Man: Thursday _____ better for me.

 Receptionist: Morning __ afternoon?

        Man: In the morning, if possible.

 Receptionist: _____ 9:15 sound?

        Man: 9:15 Thursday. That's fine.

22.   *Man:* What time _____ doctor be in today?

 Receptionist: He's here after 2:30. _____ see _____ today?

        Man: Yes. My back's killing me.

 Receptionist: The doctor's very busy, but I think we can fit you in at 5:15.

23.　　　　　*Man:* I'm Mr. Wang. _____ appointment _____ 5:15.

　　Receptionist: Please sign here. A nurse will call your name.

　　　　　　　Man: How long _____ be before I can see the doctor?

　　Receptionist: _____ with you _____ few minutes.

24.　*Receptionist:* Your appointment _____ until 2:30.

　　　　　　　Man: I know. _____ ahead _____ .

25.　　　　　*Man:* My tooth's bothering me. _____ see a doctor?

　　　　Woman: How about tomorrow? 10:30 OK?

　　　　　　　Man: _____ anything earlier?

　　　　Woman: No, but _____ call you if there's a cancellation before then.

26.　*Receptionist:* _____ your first appointment with Dr. Dans?

　　　　　　　Man: Yes, it is. _____ have a dental check-up.

　　Receptionist: Fill out this card _____ give it back to me.

　　　　　　　Man: All right. _____ pen?

27.　　　　*Student:* _____ be convenient to see you today?

　　　Professor: Yes. My office hours _____ 10:30 ___ noon.

　　　　Student: _____ trouble with the homework.

　　　Professor: Come by anytime. _____ about it.

28.　　　　*Student:* _____ Doctor Harris in?

　　　Secretary: May I have your name?

　　　　Student: Jack Stephens.

　　　Secretary: Let me check with _____ to tell _____ you're here.

29.　　　　　*Man:* Ms. McGraw. _____ Bill Sidelow from Acme Construction.

　　　　Woman: Oh, hello, Mr. Sidelow, _____ glad you called. _____ do ___ you?

　　　　　　　Man: _____ drop by today to talk over your contract.

　　　　Woman: Sure. _____ one o'clock?

　　　　　　　Man: _____ make it a little later?

　　　　Woman: Two-thirty, three?

　　　　　　　Man: Two-thirty _____ great.

　　　　Woman: Fine. _____ then.

B. Telling the Time

30.   *Man:*   What time _____ ?

           Woman: _____ a quarter to four.

           Man: Excuse me? _____ time?

           Woman: A quarter to four.

31.   *Woman:*   What time _____ ?

           Man: It's 8:15.

           Woman: _____ sure? My watch has 8:30.

           Man: Your watch must be fast.

32.   *Woman:*   _____ the time?

           Man: It's 9:05 exactly.

33.   *Man:*   What time _____ ?

           Woman: About 7:30.

34.   *Man:*   _____ what time it is?

           Woman: I'm sorry. _____ watch.

35.   *Man:*   _____ clock be right? 10:30?

           Woman: That clock is always off. _____ 11:05.

36.   *Woman:*   Check the time. _____ clock _____ kitchen.

           Man: _____ little before nine.

37.   *Woman:*   _____ late?

           Man: We will be unless we hurry.

           Woman: _____ show start?

           Man: At eight-thirty. _____ fifteen minutes to get there.

38.   *Man:*   _____ time ___ grab ___ quick bite?

           Woman: We've got thirty minutes before _____ meeting. Let's go eat.

39.   *Man:*   Come on. Let's go. The plane leaves in ten minutes.

           Woman: Let's hurry. _____ just enough time ___ make it.

40. *Man:* _____ time?

    Woman: It's about three-thirty.

    Man: Oh, no. I'm late. _____ appointment in fifteen minutes.

    Woman: _____ worry. _____ you wherever you _____ go.

41. *Man:* How long _____ on that report?

    Woman: I spent several hours on it.

42. *Man:* _____ much time in Europe?

    Woman: Oh, yes. I was there _____ four months.

43. *Woman:* _____ much time ___ get your passport?

    Man: No. It took about ten days.

3. Getting Along With People

A. Meeting and Greeting

44. *Woman:* Hi, Bill.

    Man: Hi, Jill. _____ ?

    Woman: Fine, thanks. You?

    Man: All right.

45. *Man:* Hi Margaret. _____ ?

    Woman: Really fine. How about yourself?

    Man: _____ be better, but not bad.

    Woman: Mmm. _____ good.

46. *Man-1:* Well, it seems as if _____ new here.

    Man-2: Yes. My family _____ I _____ just moved to Phoenix.

    Man-1: What type ___ business _____ in?

    Man-2: I run a management consulting firm.

47.   *Woman:* _____ in Houston long?

         Man: Two years, more or less.

    Woman: _____ like it?

         Man: The people ____ friendly _____ weather __ nice.

B. Parting

48.   *Man:* I really hate to rush off like this.

    Woman: No problem. We know _____ busy.

       Man: _____ get together again sometime soon.

49.   *Woman:* I really _____ .

       Man: Stay! Stay a little while longer.

    Woman: No. _____ too generous.

       Man: _____ sure _____ ?

    Woman: Yes. It's really getting late.

50.   *Man-1:* It's ten o'clock. _____ be leaving.

    Man-2: Leaving? Already?

    Man-1: Yes. _____ get up early tomorrow.

    Man-2: OK. Stop over again sometime.

51.   *Man:* Excuse me, Mary. _____ take off.

    Woman: OK. But _____ have another drink?

       Man: No, ____ really better not.

    Woman: All right. _____ later. Take care __ yourself.

C. Gossiping

52.   *Man:* _____ what happened to Margo?

    Woman: No, but _____ to hear ____ story.

       Man: She ____ her boss had an argument.

    Woman: _____ hear that?

       Man: Someone _____ office told me.

53.   *Woman:*   _____ the latest?

          Man: No. What's the latest?

     Woman: Mrs. Bender's _____ fired.

          Man: _____ ?

     Woman: It's not what she did; it's what she _____ do. She forgot to enter $25,000 in the company records.

          Man: _____ think her boss will forgive her?

     Woman: Not this time. _____ happened before.

54.   *Woman:*   Well, _____ know it?

          Man: Know what? _____ tell me?

     Woman: Jackie _____ quit her job, according to the newspaper.

          Man: _____ working anyway? She's rich.

     Woman: She wanted _____ to do, I guess.

          Man: With all that money, _____ have people working for her.

55.   *Man-1:*   _____ hear something interesting?

    Man-2:   Yeh. What?

    Man-1:   _____ that Tom Kelly _____ work in a zoo?

    Man-2:   No, you're kidding. _____ that?

    Man-1:   Oh, he told me about it the other day.

56.   *Woman:*   _____ John and Jill _____ get married?

          Man: _____ . Do you think they are?

     Woman: Sure. _____ together all the time?

D. Talking about the Weather

57.   *Woman:*   _____ like outside today?

          Man: It's clear _____ sunny but cold.

     Woman: _____ wear my heavy jacket.

          Man: _____ good idea.

58.   *Man:*   _____ rain today?

      Woman: I don't know. I hope so.

      Man: _____ want it to rain?

      Woman: Yes. _____ so dry lately.

59.   *Man:*   Boy, it's really a nice day today, _____ ?

      Woman: It is. Looks like spring _____ soon.

      Man: Yeh. _____ just be a few more weeks.

60.   *Woman:*   _____ stop raining?

      Man: I don't know. _____ by now.

      Woman: If this keeps up, _____ get a boat.

      Man: Oh, well. _____ always enjoyed fishing.

4. Buying Things

A. Getting Information

61.   *Man:*   What time _____ stores close?

      Woman: _____ close at six.

      Man: How about Aron's Music Shop?

      Woman: I think that's open until nine.

62. *Woman-1:*   _____ your shopping?

   Woman-2:   _____ clothes shopping __ food shopping?

   Woman-1:   Your clothes shopping.

   Woman-2:   I generally go to Damond's Department Store.

63.   *Man-1:*   _____ that sweater?

      Man-2:   I bought it at Damond's Department Store.

      Man-1:   How much _____ ?

      Man-2:   It was twenty-three dollars or something like that.

64

64. Salesman: _____ any help?

 Man: Yes. _____ pants.

 Salesman: What's your size?

 Man: Thirty waist and thirty-six inseam.

65. Woman: Excuse me. _____ help me?

 Saleswoman: Certainly. _____ ?

 Woman: _____ blouse, size 10.

 Saleswoman: _____ several over here. _____ come this way?

66. Man: Pardon me. _____ the dressing rooms?

 Saleswoman: _____ one next _____ suit rack.

 Man: _____ hold these packages ____ me?

 Saleswoman: No, but _____ behind the cash register. They'll be safe.

67. Woman: _____ keep the ice cream?

 Clerk: _____ frozen food section.

 Woman: Where's that?

 Clerk: It's two aisles _____ left _____ center _____ store.

68. Man: I can't find the instant soup.

 Clerk: _____ next _____ canned soup?

 Man: I looked there, but _____ any _____ shelf.

 Clerk: _____ try the spice section.

 _____ there.

69. Man: _____ where I can find the butter?

 Clerk: Yes. It's with dairy goods _____ store.

70. Woman: Excuse me. I can't find the canned fruit.

 Clerk: It's in aisle nine _____ fruit juices.

B. Asking Prices

71.   *Man:* How much _____ ?

It _____ price on it.

        Clerk: That book is four ninety-five. The price is on the inside cover.

72.   *Woman:* How much _____ cost?

        Clerk: They're $17.98.

      Woman: _____ think that's expensive _____ pair __ gloves?

        Clerk: Not at all. That's the best price in town.

73.   *Woman:* _____ price _____ gloves?

        Clerk: They're on sale for $18.98.

      Woman: On sale? Broadway _____ same pair for $17.98.

        Clerk: Let me look again. Oh, yes. _____ $8.98.

C. Paying for It

74.   *Man:* _____ pay for this shirt?

  Salesperson: _____ take it_____ next register.

              Man: Can't I pay ____ it here?

  Salesperson: _____ a few minutes ago, but ____ closed out for the night.

75.   *Clerk:* _____ with cash __ with a check?

      Woman: _____ possible to use a credit card?

        Clerk: No, _____ accept credit cards in this store.

76.   *Clerk:* That's twenty-nine on the bananas, fifty-three on the juice, one twenty-nine on the chicken, and eighty-nine on the milk. . . Will there be anything else?

          Man: No, that's all.

        Clerk: That's three dollars even, plus fifteen tax. . . . three fifteen.

          Man: Here's five. . . . _____ fifteen in change.

77.   *Salesman:*   So _____ like this clock radio?

           Man: Yes. _____ .

    Salesman: _____ be cash __ charge?

           Man: _____ Mastercharge.

D. Returning Items

78.   *Woman:*   _____ suppose I can return these gloves?

  Saleswoman: _____ the matter _____ ?

      Woman: _____ wrong size.

  Saleswoman: _____ before you bought _____ ?

      Woman: _____ time. The store was closing.

79.   *Woman:*   _____ return these gloves?

  Salesperson: _____ on sale?

      Woman: Yes, but _____ too small.

  Salesperson: I'm sorry. Sales on sale items are final.

      Woman: Let me talk _____ manager.

  Salesperson: I am the manager, ma'am.

80.   *Woman:*   Pardon me. I received these gloves as a gift. _____ too small.

    Salesman: _____ from this Broadway store?

      Woman: I'm pretty sure. _____ sell this item?

    Salesman: Yes, we do. We can't give you a cash return, but we can give you a credit voucher.

      Woman: _____ fine. I think you sell these gloves for $17.98.

    Salesman: That's right. Here's your voucher. It's good ____ $17.98 on any store purchase.

81.   *Man:*   _____ return this radio.

  Salesperson: What seems to be the problem?

        Man: The dial is broken. _____ turn.

  Salesperson: We can replace it for you. _____ your receipt?

82.   *Woman:* I'd like to return this record. _____ scratch on it.

Salesperson: I'm sorry. We can't refund ___ replace records.

   Woman: But _____ scratch on it.

Salesperson: I'm sorry. _____ the store policy.

5. Eating and Drinking

A. Arriving

83.   *Man:* _____ reservations _____ party ___ six.

   Woman: What's your name?

   Man: My name is George McClintock.

   Woman: Yes, sir. If you'll come this way, _____ you to your table.

84.   *Man:* I'd like to make reservations _____ 8:00 tonight.

   Woman: _____ in your group?

   Man: _____ .

   Woman: _____ name _____ party please?

   Man: Hill.

   Woman: That's Hill, party ___ two, 8:00 Saturday.

85.   *Woman:* Good evening. _____ in your party?

   Man: _____ four ___ us.

   Woman: _____ your name please?

   Man: Bryant. B-R-Y-A-N-T.

   Woman: OK, Mr. Bryant. _____ short wait. If _____ like to wait in the lounge, we'll give you a call.

B. Ordering

86.   *Hostess:* Good evening. _____ here for dinner _____ just cocktails.

   Man: _____ just for drinks.

   Hostess: Fine. The cocktail lounge is to your right.

87.   *Man:*   Waiter, _____ a bar list?

        Waiter: Yes, here you are. _____ this evening?

        Man: What's the bar special?

        Waiter: Tonight, it's double scotch on the rocks.

88.   *Woman:*   _____ drink, sir?

        Man: Make that a gin and tonic.

        Woman: _____ anything else?

        Man: Yes, could you bring us some nuts.

89.   *Man:*   Bartender, _____ draft beer?

        Bartender: Sure. We have Bud _____ Coors on tap.

        Man: _____ Bud.

90.   *Woman:*   Waiter, we'd like to order now.

        Waiter: Yes? _____ like to begin with?

        Woman: Which salad _____ recommend?

        Waiter: I'd suggest the Chef's delight.

        Woman: _____ cheese in it?

        Waiter: Yes, it does. _____ always _____ favorite with our customers.

91.   *Waitress:* May I take your order please?

        Man: Yes, I'd like the prime rib dinner.

        Waitress: That comes with potatoes. Would you like a baked potato _____ french fries?

        Man: Baked potato.

        Waitress: _____ dressing would you like on your salad?

        Man: _____?

        Waitress: Italian, French, and Blue Cheese.

        Man: I'll have Italian.

92.   *Waitress:* _____ your dinner, sir?

        Man: It's just fine.

        Waitress: _____ ?

        Man: No, thanks. Everything's fine.

69

93.   *Woman:* I think _____ just have coffee.

           Waitress: _____ anything else?

           Woman: No, _____ . Thank you.

           Waitress: Here's your check.

94.   *Man:* _____ bring us our check, please?

           Waitress: Yes, sir. Right away.

C. Problems with the Food

95.   *Man:* Waiter, this steak _____ cooked longer.

         Waiter: _____ order it?

         Man: Medium rare, but _____ practically raw!

         Waiter: Well, I'll return it and bring you another.

96.   *Waitress:* Yes, _____ something wrong?

         Man: I think _____ mistake. This isn't what I ordered.

    Waitress: I'm sorry. _____ confused orders.

97.   *Woman:* Waiter, _____ for a second please?

         Waiter: What's the problem, ma'am?

         Woman: This soup is cold.

         Waiter: I'm sorry. _____ a hot one.

D. Fast Food

98.   *Woman:* Next. May I help you?

         Man: Yeh. _____ superburger, fries, _____ large coke.

        Woman: Super, fries, large coke. _____ dollar twenty-seven.

99.   *Man:*   Who's next?

   Woman: _____ order of french fries _____ small coke.

   Man: Anything else?

   Woman: No, that's all.

   Man: How about __ hamburger _____ apple pie?

   Woman: No, just french fries _____ small coke.

   Man: OK. _____ fifty-nine cents.

100.   *Woman:*   Yes, sir. _____ you?

   Man: Two hamburgers _____ french fries.

   Woman: _____ anything else?

   Man: No, that's it.

   Woman: _____ to go _____ eat here?

   Man: _____ eating here.

101.   *Man:*   _____ any ketchup?

   Woman: It's on the service counter.

   Man: _____ keep the salt ____ pepper?

   Woman: _____ find it in the same place.

6. Talking at School

A. In the Classroom

102.   *Student:*   _____ this word.

   Teacher: _____ "apricot"?

   Student: Yes. _____ say it in Spanish?

   Teacher: I don't know. _____ Spanish.

103.   *Student-1:*   _____ "mañana" in English?

   Student-2: I think the word is "tomorrow" in English.

104.   *Student:*   _____ meaning _____ word?

   Teacher: What word _____ about?

   Student: _____ the meaning ____ this word "split."

   Teacher: It means "to divide."

105. Student-1: _____ translate this sentence into Chinese?

Student-2: What's the sentence?

Student-1: "The more, the merrier."

Student-2: _____ no idea.

106. Student: _____ repeat that answer again please?

Teacher: Yes. The correct answer is "B".

Student: _____ "B" or "D"?

Teacher: "B" as in "boy."

107. Student: _____ with this problem?

Teacher: What's the problem?

Student: _____ much math _____ this problem requires trigonometry.

Teacher: Let's see. That's not too difficult. Let me give you ___ hand.

108. Student-1: _____ our new teacher. _____ ?

Student-2: Oh, he's not too bad. _____ worse teachers.

Student-1: _____ give us too much homework?

Student-2: Yeh. He does give us _____ .

109. Student-1: This class is awfully big, _____ ?

Student-2: Yeh. _____ too many students.

Student-1: _____ signed up _____ different class.

Student-2: Right. You can learn more in smaller classes.

110. Student-1: Hey, John. _____ in the lab yesterday?

Student-2: No, _____ make it. _____ there either?

Student-1: No, I wasn't. Darn. _____ you could tell me the assignment.

Student-2: I guess _____ get it from somebody else.

111. Student: _____ best place _____ good dictionary?

Teacher: _____ tried the campus bookstore?

Student: Yes. But the ones there are not English-English dictionaries.

Teacher: Then, _____ get one at Blue _____ Gray Bookstore.

72

7. Apartment Living

A. Finding a Place to Live

112. *Woman:* Excuse me. _____ any vancancies?

   Man: No, we don't. _____ the sign out front?

   Woman: No, _____ sign.

   Man: Well, _____ any vacancies until May 1.

113. *Man:* _____ about the ad _____ apartment.

   Woman: The apartment's still available.

   Man: _____ the rent?

   Woman: It's $170 per month.

   Man: _____ include utilities?

   Woman: Yes, _____ included.

114. *Woman:* _____ sign a lease for this apartment?

   Man: No, you don't, but _____ deposit.

   Woman: _____ deposit refundable?

   Man: Oh, yes. _____ get it back when you leave.

115. *Woman:* _____ apartments two-bedroom apartments?

   Man: No. _____ one-bedroom ____ studio apartments.

   Woman: What's the difference in price?

   Man: Two bedrooms are two thirty, one-bedrooms are two ten, ____ studios are one eighty.

116. *Man:* _____ lease on your apartment?

   Woman: Yes, our landlord _____ us a year's lease.

   Man: _____ your new place?

   Woman: Yes, it's got all the modern conveniences.

B. Getting a Phone

117. *Woman:* Hello. My name is Mary Alvero. _____ phone put
       in my new apartment.

      Man: _____ your apartment, Miss Alvero?

      Woman: 1107 East Alto Avenue, Apartment 5.

      Man: _____ send someone out a week from Thursday.

118. *Man:* _____ a phone installed in my home.

      Woman: _____ many long distance calls?

      Man: Yes, we do. We make quite _____ .

      Woman: Then _____ ask for a large deposit.

119. *Man:* South Central Bell. May I help you?

      Woman: Yes, _____ install a phone in my apartment.

      Man: _____ had previous service with us?

      Woman: No, _____ . I'm new here.

120. *Woman:* _____ to put down a deposit?

      Man: Yes, _____ be $50. It's refundable.

      Woman: _____ the deposit?

      Man: _____ come to our office on Main Street.

C. Problems

121. *Woman:* Excuse me. I hate to disturb you, but . . . .

      Man: You're the new tenant in twelve-B, _____ ?

      Woman: That's right. _____ problem with the toilet.

      It _____ stop flushing.

      Man: OK. Just a minute. _____ up _____ take a look.

74

122. **Woman:** Hi. _____ check _____ this month's rent.

   Man: Wait a minute. _____ receipt.

   By the way, _____ any problems in your apartment?

   Woman: Well, as a matter _____ fact, the heater _____ work too well,

   _____ garbage disposal is broken.

   Man: Hmmm. _____ look into those things sometime this week.

123. **Woman:** Oh, no! Not again!

   Man: What's wrong? _____ the matter with _____ sink?

   Woman: Yes, it's gotten stopped up again.

   Man: I guess _____ plumber.

124. **Woman 1:** The landlord wants to raise my rent again.

   Woman 2: _____ why?

   Woman 1: He says that it's because of inflation.

   Woman 2: Well, _____ housing authorities if I _____ you.

8. Taking Care of Business

A. At the Post Office

125. **Woman:** _____ mail this letter overseas.

   Clerk: That's 31¢ per half ounce for overseas mail.

   Woman: That's expensive. _____ aerograms?

   Clerk: They're twenty-two cents _____ .

126. **Man:** _____ for a letter to get to Iran?

   Clerk: It'll take five or six days.

   Man: _____ register it.

   Clerk: All right. _____ probably take a little longer to get there though.

127. **Woman:** _____ to get a post office box?

     Clerk: Certainly. Fill out this form.

    Woman: _____ ?

     Clerk: It's twenty dollars per year.

128. **Clerk:** Next, please. I can help you down here.

    Woman: I'd like four aerograms _____ three thirteen-cent stamps.

     Clerk: _____ three aerograms and four stamps?

    Woman: No, the other way around.

B. At the Bank

129. **Man:** _____ a savings _____ checking account.

    Woman: Our minimum deposit _____ savings account is $25.

     Man: What is the interest rate?

    Woman: It's 4 1/2%.

     Man: _____ charge _____ checks?

    Woman: Each check that you write _____ 20¢.

130. **Woman:** _____ withdraw some money from my savings account.

    Teller: First _____ fill out _____ withdrawal forms.

    Woman: Oh, no. It _____ my account number. I forgot my bank book.

    Teller: I'm afraid _____ that first.

131. **Man:** _____ cash a check here?

    Teller: _____ an account with us?

    Man: Yes, _____ checking account here.

    Teller: Please write your account number _____ .

    Man: _____ all you need?

    Teller: _____ see one more piece of identification?

    Man: _____ driver's license do?

    Teller: Yes. _____ fine.

132.   *Man:* _____ ask about _____ out a loan.

     Loan Officer: Do you have an account here?

     Man: Yes, _____ customer here for several months.

     Loan Officer: _____ borrow?

     Man: Three thousand dollars.

C. Auto Repair

133.   *Attendant:* Yes, sir. May I help you?

     Man: _____ it up with regular?

     Attendant: Sure. _____ to check ____ oil ____ water?

     Man: If you would please.

134.   *Woman:* _____ check my battery?

     Attendant: _____ problem?

     Woman: The car is hard to start.

     Attendant: Hmm. The battery seems OK. Maybe something else is wrong.

135.   *Man:* _____ anything wrong with the car?

     Attendant: Not really. You just need a tune-up.

     Man: _____ expensive?

     Attendant: It'll cost $23.50.

     Man: _____ get to it?

     Attendant: If you leave the car now, I can finish it by five today.

136.   *Woman:* _____ what the problem is?

     Mechanic: Yep. You need a new carburetor and fuel pump.

     Woman: _____ replace _____ ?

     Mechanic: Absolutely. There's no other way.

     Woman: I think I'll get a second opinion.

D. Immigration

137. *Immigration Officer:* How long _____ be in the United States?

    Woman: Just _____ months.

    Immigration Officer: What's your reason _____ to go?

    Woman: I'm going as a tourist.

    Immigration Officer: _____ relatives in the U.S.?

    Woman: Yes. My son's a student at the University of California.

138. *Officer:* What _____ visa _____ ?

    Man: It's a student visa.

    Officer: _____ the United States?

    Man: I came into the country on August 6th.

    Officer: _____ your port of entry?

    Man: New York City, Kennedy Airport.

139. *Officer:* Mister VanHoff. We understand that _____ school.

    Man: No, _____ , but _____ sick recently.

    Officer: _____ attended only three days since last July.

    Man: Three days? No, _____ more than that.

    Officer: _____ take away your visa.

140. *Officer:* Number forty-six?

    Woman: That's me. I have a problem. _____ my visa.

    Officer: _____ see Miss Vance. _____ at two.

    Woman: But _____ here all morning.

141. *Man:* I would like to extend my visa.

    Officer: _____ on a tourist visa _____ student visa?

    Man: It's an F-1 visa.

    Officer: We'll need a letter from your school _____ financial statement from you.

E. At the Doctor's Office

142.   *Nurse:* The doctor _____ see you now. Come this way.

           Man: _____ examination room?

           Nurse: It's to your right. You can lie down _____ table.

143.   *Doctor:* What seems to be the problem, Mrs. Allen?

          Woman: _____ pains in my chest recently.

          Doctor: _____ difficulty breathing.

          Woman: Sometimes. But not too much.

          Doctor: Well, let's take an X-Ray _____ your chest.

144.   *Doctor:* Here's a prescription. I'd like you to take _____ pills three times a day.

         Patient: _____ anything else I should do?

         Doctor: Yes. You should drink _____ liquids and get _____ rest.

         Patient: OK. _____ pharmacy in this building?

         Doctor: No, but you can have that prescription filled at any drugstore.

145.   *Doctor:* You're suffering from an allergy.

         Patient: _____ serious?

         Doctor: No. I'll just give you a prescription.

         Patient: _____ the medicine?

         Doctor: _____ pharmacy in this building.

F. At the Barber Shop

146. *Customer:* I'd like to get a haircut, please.

          Barber: _____ cut?

      Customer: _____ cut it too short. Just trim it.

          Barber: _____ shampoo your hair also?

      Customer: Yes. _____ good idea.

147. *Hairdresser:* How would you like your hair cut?

    Woman: _____ too long, but _____ cut it too much.

    Hairdresser: _____ want me to shape it?

    Woman: Yes, please do.

9. Staying at Hotels and Motels

148.   *Man:* I'd like a room for the night, please.

    Clerk: How many people _____ your party?

    Man: _____ —my wife and myself.

    Clerk: We have a double _____ sixteen dollars.

149.   *Woman:* How much is a room for one night?

    Clerk: It's $14 _____ single and $16 _____ double.

    Woman: _____ include tax?

    Clerk: No, the tax is extra.

150.   *Clerk:* _____ us in advance?

    Man: Yes. I made a reservation two weeks ago.

    Clerk: Well, _____ your reservation card.

    Man: Would you please check again.

    Clerk: I'm sorry. I still _____ .

151.   *Clerk:* _____ your name, sir?

    Man: Albert Johnson. I called ahead two hours ago.

    Clerk: Oh, yes. Your room is 213. Here's your key.

    Man: _____ ?

    Clerk: You can pay when you check out.

152.   *Woman:* _____ any vacancies?

    Clerk: I'm sorry, ma'am. We're completely booked.

    Woman: _____ a reservation.

    Clerk: That _____ .

153. Man: _____ reservations for this weekend.

Clerk: _____ your name, sir?

Man: Johnson. I called yesterday.

Clerk: Yes. _____ your reservation card.

154. Woman: _____ get _____ ?

Clerk: There's a restaurant in the lobby.

Woman: _____ food to the room?

Clerk: Yes, we do. All you _____ is dial room service.

155. Clerk: Your room is 1456. It's on the fourteenth floor.

Man: _____ place have an elevator?

Clerk: It does, but _____ repaired right now.

156. Man: _____ any messages for me—Mr. Jackson?

Clerk: Let me check the box. No, _____ any messages.

157. Woman: _____ hotel have a sauna?

Clerk: Yes, there's a sauna and a steam room.

Woman: _____ located?

Clerk: _____ are through the lobby toward the pool area.

158. Woman: _____ phone in the room?

Clerk: _____ have phones.

Woman: _____ to make a call?

Clerk: Yes. We charge 25¢ for each call.

159. Man: Is there a televsion _____ ?

Clerk: No, _____ . _____ like one?

Man: Yes, I would. _____ per day?

Clerk: It's two dollars a day extra.

160. Woman: Is there __ public telephone here?

Clerk: There's one across _____ lobby.

Woman: I need _____ make __ long distance call.

Clerk: You can do that from your room. We'll add it _____ your bill.

161. **Clerk:** Room Service. May I help you?

Woman: Please send some toast _____ coffee up to Room 212.

Clerk: _____ , ma'am?

Woman: Yes, that's all.

162. **Clerk:** Good morning. _____ well last night?

Woman: Yes. The room was fine.

Clerk: _____ out this morning?

Woman: Yes, _____ around ten.

163. **Clerk:** _____ pay the bill?

Man: Excuse me?

Clerk: You can pay with cash _____ check _____ with a credit card.

Man: _____ put it on my credit card.

164. **Woman:** _____ to the airport from here?

Clerk: There's a bus from _____ airport every half hour.

Woman: _____ taxi stand nearby?

Clerk: No, but I can call one for you.

10. Social Situations

A. Questions and Invitations

165. **Woman:** _____ last night?

Man: I just stayed home.

Woman: _____ to the concert?

Man: _____ , but then I decided not to.

166. **Man:** _____ anything over the weekend?

Woman: Not much. _____ ?

Man: _____ to go skiing, but I wound up studying.

167. Man-1: _____ this weekend?

Man-2: I have _____ studying to do.

Man-1: _____ go camping with us?

Man-2: To tell you the truth, I really _____ to camp.

168. Woman: Mark, _____ come over for dinner tomorrow night?

Man: Oh, wow. That's nice. What time _____ come by?

Woman: Around seven _____ seven-thirty.

Man: Great. _____ anything?

Woman: You could bring _____ wine if _____ like.

169. Man: Would you like to join us _____ dinner tonight?

Woman: _____ . What time should I come over?

Man: We're planning dinner _____ eight o'clock.

Woman: _____ dress?

Man: _____ informal. You can come as you are.

170. Man: _____ pay us a visit about nine tonight?

Woman: What's the occasion?

Man: _____ Gloria's birthday _____ having _____ friends over.

Woman: Should I bring a gift?

Man: Oh, no. _____ simple get-together.

171. Man: Let's take in a concert tonight.

Woman: Good. _____ really like to hear some music.

Man: And afterward we could go someplace quiet _____ a drink.

Woman: That sounds like a nice way _____ spend the evening.

172. Woman-1: Hello.

Woman-2: Jean, _____ Ellen.

Woman-1: Hi, Ellen. _____ ?

Woman-2: Fine. Say, I wonder if _____ catch a film with me tonight.

Woman-1: What film _____ ?

Woman-2: The House of Horrors—it's a thriller.

83

173.   *Woman:*   Hello.

       Man: Hello, Jane. This is Pete. It's such a nice day today that I thought we might go to the zoo.

       Woman: I wish _____ me earlier. _____ just made plans to play tennis.

       Man: Oh, that's too bad. Maybe some other time.

       Woman: OK, Pete. Thanks _____ .

174.   *Man:*   _____ like to go out tonight?

       Woman: Great. _____ have in mind?

       Man: I thought we could see _____ new play _____ university.

       Woman: That sounds good. I hope we can get tickets.

175.   *Man-1:*   Hey, _____ this afternoon?

       Man-2:   Nothing special. Why?

       Man-1:   Let's get together _____ beer _____ two.

176.   *Man:*   There's a street festival in Scottsdale this coming Saturday. _____ ?

       Woman: Sure. _____ OK if we take your car?

       Man: Fine. _____ leave around ten?

       Woman: That's good. If we don't leave early, _____ parking space.

11. Talking on the Telephone

A. Taking Messages

177.   *Woman:*   Hello.

       Man: Is Mary there, please?

       Woman: No, she's out right now.

       Man: _____ be back?

       Woman: I'm not sure—probably around six. Who _____ called?

       Man: This is Bill Jackson. _____ back this evening.

178.   *Woman:*   Hello.

    Man: Hello. Is Bob at home?

   Woman: _____ . May I take a message?

    Man: Yes. _____ George called.

179.   *Woman:*   Hilton Hotel. May I help you?

    Man: Mr. John Thomas. Room 213 please.

   Woman: ____ connect you. Mr. Thomas _____ at the moment.

    Man: May I leave a message?

   Woman: Certainly. _____ message?

    Man: _____ call Alex Green at 273-7928. _____ .

180.   *Man:*   Hello.

   Woman: Is Mary at home?

    Man: _____ . _____ message?

   Woman: Please. This is Natalie Henderson. _____ ?

    Man: Sure. _____ your number?

   Woman: _____ . Maybe _____ write it down. It's 773-5641.

B. Getting Information

181.   *Woman:*   Information. May I help you?

    Man: Yes. _____ trouble calling ____ Bookshelf Bookstore.

   Woman: _____ dialing?

    Man: 482-9736.

   Woman: Sir, the number _____ to 978-8226.

182.   *Man:*   Information. Operator number thirteen. _____ ?

   Woman: _____ the number of Ace Car Rental in Phoenix?

    Man: Just a moment please. That number is 834-2170.

   Woman: 2170. OK. Thank you.

183.   *Woman:* Information. What city please?

          Man: Bakersfield.

    Woman: What number _____ ?

          Man: I need _____ Bill Jackson, J-A-C-K-S-O-N. He lives on Market Street.

    Woman: _____ Bill Jackson _____ Gill Jackson?

          Man: Bill. That's "B" as in "boy."

    Woman: The number is 761-4688.

184.   *Man:* Information. Operator 37.

    Woman: _____ a listing for Sam Johnson?

          Man: _____ the address?

    Woman: I believe he lives on Parkway Boulevard.

          Man: I'm sorry. _____ Sam Johnson on Parkway.

185.   *Man-1:* Information. What number _____ ?

    Man-2: I need the number _____ German Embassy in Los Angeles.

    Man-1: _____ dial information in Los Angeles. Dial 1-213-555-1212.

    Man-2: Right. Thanks.

C. Long Distance Calls

186.   *Man:* Hello.

    Operator: _____ collect call from Pedro Salazar. _____ accept the charges?

          Man: Sure. Put _____ on.

187. *Operator:* Operator.

    Woman: Operator, _____ 274-1347.

    Operaotr: That number _____ outside _____ zone. _____ dollar thirty _____ three minutes.

    Woman: All right. _____ put in the coins.

188. Operator: Overseas Operator. Which country?

         Man: Iran.

   Operator: Yes, go ahead.

         Man: _____ book a call _____ Tehran, Iran.

   Operator: For which date _____ time?

         Man: March twenty-first at three p.m.

   Operator: _____ your name _____ phone number?

         Man: Mike James at 964-5397. The number in Iran is 827-803.

   Operator: _____ when your call is ready to go through.

189. Operator: Overseas Operator.

    Woman: _____ place a call _____ France.

   Operator: Your number please?

    Woman: Area code 513, number 433-5009.

   Operator: Which city in France?

    Woman: Paris. The number is 924896.

   Operator: Your call is ready. Go ahead.

D. Wrong Numbers and Unwanted Calls

190.   Man: Hello.

    Woman: Hello. May I speak to Jim?

      Man: I'm afraid _____ wrong number.

    Woman: _____ 278-2001?

      Man: No, _____ 278-2010.

191.   Woman: Hello.

      Man: Hello. Is Bob in?

    Woman: There's no Bob here. _____ ?

      Man: _____ reach Robert Brown at 789-8307.

    Woman: That's our number, but _____ mistake.

               _____ check his listing again.

      Man: I'll do that. Sorry for disturbing you.

192. Woman: Hello. Cowden residence.

 Man: _____ Mrs. Cowden?

 Woman: Yes, it is.

 Man: Mrs. Cowden, I represent a company with a fine line of household cleansers and our company representative _____ in your neighborhood soon _____ stop by to show . . . .

 Woman: _____ . I'm afraid I already have all the cleansers I need.

193. Man: Hello.

 Woman: Hello. _____ Jackson residence?

 Man: Yes, it is . . .

 Woman: We understand that _____ recently purchased a home.

 Man: That's correct.

 Woman: Well, Mr. Jackson, I represent the Acme Water Purification System Company, and as you know . . . .

 Man: I'm sorry. I'm not interested.

12. Making Excuses

194. Woman: _____ me last night, _____ ?

 Man: Yes. I called several times but _____ .

 Woman: I was home all night. _____ dialed the wrong number.

195. Woman: Bob, where were you yesterday? We had a meeting.

 Man: _____ supposed to come _____ meeting?

 Woman: Yes. The meeting was for the entire group.

 Man: Oh, I'm sorry. _____ that.

196. Man: Hi, honey.

 Woman: _____ ? It's nine o'clock already.

 Man: _____ work late tonight.

 Woman: Well, _____

197. Man-1: _____ typing that report for me?

Man-2: Not yet.

Man-1: But I gave it to you yesterday morning.

Man-2: I know, but _____ very busy.

198. Woman: _____ so late?

Man: _____ flat tire on the way over here.

Woman: But the party's almost over.

Man: Oh, that's too bad. _____ any food left?

199. Woman-1: Meyers Cotton Company.

Woman-2: Miss Davis, _____ Jean Thompson. I can't come in to work

_____ .

Woman-1: What's the problem? _____ ?

Woman-2: No. My grandmother died and _____ for the funeral.

200. Man-1: How about _____ over to our place _____ dinner this weekend?

Man-2: Friday _____ Saturday?

Man-1: _____ Saturday night around seven _____ so?

Man-2: Oh, no. We already have plans for Saturday.

PART THREE

ACTIVATION
EXERCISES

Activation Exercises

1. Getting There

A. At the Airport

1. Ask the agent if his airline has flights for (Hawaii/Boston).
2. Ask the airlines agent when there are flights for (Las Vegas/Atlanta).
3. Ask him what time the flight arrives in (Las Vegas/Atlanta).
4. Tell the agent that you want to fly (coach/first class).
5. Tell the agent you would like to buy a ticket for the (9:30 AM/3:30 PM) flight on (Saturday/Wednesday).
6. Ask the agent where the departure gate is.
7. Ask him if the flight to (St. Louis/Hong Kong) is scheduled to leave on time.
8. Ask the agent why the flight from (Denver/London) has been delayed.

B. Buses

1. Ask the driver if the bus goes downtown.
2. Ask the driver if he has change for a dollar.
3. Tell the driver that you need a transfer ticket.
4. Ask the driver if you should transfer to the number seven bus or to the number seventeen bus.
5. Ask him how long it takes to get (downtown/to the bus terminal).
6. Tell the driver you need to get off at Fourth Street.
7. Tell the driver to let you off at the next stop.
8. Ask another passenger if the seat beside him is taken.
9. Tell the passenger you're not sure where to get off the bus.
10. Offer your seat to an old man who has just got on the bus.

C. Taxis

1. Ask the taxi driver about how much the fare will be to (the airport/the Italian Consulate).
2. Tell the driver you're going to (44th Street and Broadway/Fifth Avenue and Washington Street).
3. Ask the driver if he's been a cab driver for long.
4. Ask him if he can suggest a good place to eat.
5. Ask him how much the fare is.
6. Tell the driver to keep the change.
7. Call the cab company. Tell the person on the phone to send a cab to your hotel. Give your hotel address.

D. Renting a Car

1. Ask the agent how many different kinds of cars are available.
2. Ask her which one is the least expensive.
3. Tell the agent you will need a car for three days.
4. Ask her if she would like to see your driver's license.
5. Ask her if you have to have a credit card in order to rent a car.

E. Getting Directions

1. Tell _____ how to get to your house.
2. Ask _____ how you get to (the Student Union/City Hall).
3. Ask _____ where the nearest bus stop is.
4. Ask _____ if (Fifth Street/Adams Street) is north or south of (Van Buren Street/ Washington Street).
5. Ask _____ how long it takes to walk to the post office.
6. Ask _____ if the post office is on the east or west side of the street.
7. Tell _____ you appreciate her help.

2. As Time Goes By

A. Making Appointments

1. Call a dentist's office. Tell the receptionist you would like to make an appointment to see the dentist.
2. Ask the receptionist if the dentist is available on Tuesday or Wednesday.
3. Tell the receptionist that (your tooth is bothering you/you would like to have your teeth cleaned and checked).
4. Call a theatre. Ask the person what movie is showing tonight.
5. Ask the theatre person what time the movie begins.
6. You are a student. Make an appointment with your teacher to talk about an assignment.
7. Ask the teacher if it'd be convenient to meet her today. Tell her why you would like to meet.

B. Telling the Time

1. Ask _____ what time it is.
2. There's a concert tonight. Ask _____ when it begins.
3. Ask _____ if it's 1:00 yet.
4. Ask _____ how long it is before the next class begins.
5. Tell _____ to hurry up. Give a reason.
6. Ask _____ how much time he spent on his homework.

7. Ask _____ how long it takes to drive to (Cleveland/Portland).

8. Ask _____ if it took a long time to get his passport.

9. Tell _____ when you will pick him up tomorrow.

10. Ask _____ what the time is now in (Japan/Turkey).

3. Getting Along With People

A. Meeting and Greeting

1. It's morning. Say good morning to _____ and ask him how he is.

2. You meet someone new. Ask him how long he has been in (town/this English program).

3. Ask him what he does for a living.

4. Ask him how he likes (the United States/his classes).

5. Tell _____ why you like (California/Vermont).

6. Tell _____ why you like (Texas/New York) more than (California/Arizona).

7. Ask _____ what kind of business he's in.

8. Tell _____ that you're planning to move to (Bogota/Washington) next year.

9. Ask _____ about his family.

B. Parting

1. Tell your friend that you'd like to get together soon.

2. Say good-bye to your friend.

3. Thank your friend for his hospitality.

4. Ask _____ if he'd like another drink.

5. Tell a friend that you have to leave. Give a reason.

C. Gossiping

1. Ask _____ if he heard what happened to (Juan/Abdul).

2. Tell _____ what happened to (Juan/Abdul).

3. Ask _____ if he wants to hear something interesting.

4. Tell _____ some news.

5. Ask _____ if he thinks (Juan/Abdul) will get married soon.

6. Tell _____ that you really don't want to talk about it.

D. Talking about the Weather

1. Ask _____ what the weather is like today.

2. Ask _____ if it's warm or cool today.

3. Ask _____ if she thinks it's going to rain today.

4. Tell _____ that it looks like (spring/fall) is coming soon.

5. Ask _____ if she likes (spring/fall).
6. Ask _____ which season she prefers. Ask her why.
7. Complain about the weather.

4. Buying Things

A. Getting Information

1. Ask _____ what time the bookstore closes.
2. Ask _____ whether or not the library is open on weekends.
3. Ask _____ where he does his shopping.
4. Ask _____ where he bought his shirt.
5. You're in a department store. Ask the clerk for some help.
6. Ask him if he thinks a size (15-32/14-31) shirt will fit you.
7. Ask the clerk where the dressing room is.
8. You're in a grocery store. Ask a clerk where the (frozen food/dairy) section is.

B. Asking Prices

1. You're in a bookstore. Ask a clerk how much (your English textbook/a notebook) costs.
2. Tell the clerk that you think the (textbook/dictionary) is too expensive.
3. You're in a department store. Ask a clerk if (gloves/shoes) are on sale.
4. Ask the clerk if the store gives discounts for students.

C. Paying for It.

1. Ask a clerk where you can pay for your purchase.
2. Ask a clerk if it is possible to use a credit card.
3. Tell the clerk you would like to buy (this book/some pencils).
4. Ask the clerk how much the sales tax is.

D. Returning Items

1. Ask the clerk if you can return (a record/a shirt).
2. Tell the clerk why you want to return (the record/the shirt).
3. Ask a clerk to let you speak to the manager.
4. You're a dissatisfied customer. Complain about a purchase you made.

5. Eating and Drinking

A. Arriving

1. You arrive at a restaurant. Tell the head waiter how many people are in your party.
2. The headwaiter asks you your name. Pronounce your name and spell it for him.
3. Ask him if you will have to wait long.
4. Ask him if it's all right if you wait in the lounge.

B. Ordering

1. You're a customer. Ask the waiter to bring you a menu.
2. Ask the waiter what he recommends.
3. Ask the bartender to give you a beer.
4. Order something to eat.
5. Ask the waiter for your check.

C. Problems with the Food

1. Ask the waiter to come to your table.
2. Tell the waiter you think he's (made a mistake/confused orders).
3. Tell the waiter your steak should have been cooked more.
4. Tell the waiter that your soup is cold.
5. Complain to a waiter about your (food/drink).

D. Fast Food

1. You're a customer. Tell a clerk you want a (hamburger/superburger) and a (small coke/large coffee).
2. Ask a clerk where the (ketchup/salt and pepper) is.
3. Tell the clerk to put your food in a bag.

6. Talking at School

1. Ask _____ how to say _____ in English.
2. Ask _____ how he would translate "let's go" into (Spanish/Farsi).
3. Ask the teacher to repeat what he just said.
4. Ask _____ what the meaning of _____ is.
5. Ask _____ if he came to school yesterday.
6. Ask _____ if he likes your English teacher.
7. Ask _____ what he thinks of the class.
8. Ask _____ if he's done the homework.

9. Ask the teacher if he said ("B"/14) or ("D"/40)
10. Ask the teacher where to buy the textbook.
11. You don't know the meaning of an expression. Ask the teacher to explain it to you.
12. Ask the teacher to help you with a problem.

7. Apartment Living

A. Finding a Place to Live

1. Ask the manager if there are any vacancies.
2. Ask him how much the rent is.
3. Ask him if you have to sign a lease.
4. Ask him if the utilities are included in the rent.
5. Ask him when you have to pay the rent.
6. Ask him if you have to put down a deposit.

B. Getting a Phone

1. You are a new tenant. Call the phone company. Tell the clerk you would like to have a phone installed. Give your name and address.
2. Ask the clerk if you have to put down a deposit.
3. Ask the clerk when the phone will be installed.
4. Ask the clerk the cost of the phone service.

C. Problems

1. Tell the landlord you are having a problem with the (sink/toilet).
2. Tell him your (heater/air conditioner) doesn't work.
3. Tell him if he doesn't fix the (stove/door), you'll (refuse to pay the rent/move out).
4. Ask the landlord if he can fix your (garbage disposal/door lock).
5. Ask the landlord why the rent is being raised.
6. Describe to the landlord a problem you are having with your apartment.
7. Your neighbors are making too much noise. Ask them to be a little quieter.

8. Taking Care of Business

A. At the Post Office

1. Tell the clerk you want to mail a letter overseas.
2. Ask the clerk how much aerograms are.
3. Ask the clerk how long it takes a letter to get to (Kuwait/Korea).
4. Tell the clerk that you want (five/ten) 13-cent stamps and (six/eight) 31-cent stamps.

5. Tell the clerk you would like to apply for a post office box.

B. At the Bank

1. Tell the teller that you want to open a (savings/checking) account.
2. Ask what the interest rate is.
3. Ask the teller to check how much money is in your checking account.
4. Tell him you would like to withdraw some money from your savings account.
5. Ask the teller if you can cash a check.
6. Inquire about taking out a loan.

C. Auto Repair

1. Tell the gas station attendant to give you (two/three) dollars worth of (regular/unleaded/premium).
2. Ask the attendant to check your oil and water.
3. Ask the attendant if there's anything wrong with the car.
4. Ask the attendant if he can give your car a tune-up.
5. Ask him how long it will take to fix your car.
6. Ask him about how much the repairs will cost.
7. Explain a mechanical problem with your car.

D. Immigration

1. Talk to the immigration officer. Tell him how long you intend to be in the United States.
2. Tell him your reason for wanting to go to the U.S.
3. Tell the officer that you'd like to extend your visa.
4. Tell the officer that you've lost your visa. Ask him what you have to do.
5. Ask _____ whether he's on a tourist or student visa.
6. Explain to the immigration officer why you haven't attended class recently.
7. Explain to an immigration officer why you want a visa.
8. Briefly tell about a problem you've had with immigration.

E. At the Doctor's Office

1. Tell the doctor you're having trouble (eating/sleeping/breathing/seeing).
2. Ask the doctor what kind of medicine he's going to give you.
3. Ask the doctor where you can get the medicine.
4. Ask the doctor if your problem is serious.
5. Describe your health problem to a doctor.

F. At the Barber Shop

1. Tell the barber you'd like a haircut.
2. Tell him to cut (a little/a lot).
3. Ask him to (trim/shampoo/shape) your hair.

9. Staying at Hotels and Motels

1. Ask the clerk if there are any vacancies.
2. Ask the clerk the price of a (single/double) room.
3. Ask the clerk if there's a restaurant nearby.
4. Ask the clerk if the elevator works.
5. Ask the clerk if there's a (telephone/television) in the room.
6. Ask the clerk when you should pay your bill.
7. Tell the clerk you have made a reservation.
8. Ask the clerk if there have been any messages for you.
9. Dial room service. Ask for something to eat.
10. You arrive at a hotel. The hotel has lost your reservation card. There is no room for you. Complain about this situation.
11. You return to your hotel room. You find that your camera is missing. Report this to the manager.
12. You have been in a hotel for two weeks. Your room is on the fourteenth floor. The elevator has not been repaired. Talk to the manager.

10. Social Situations

1. Ask _____ what he did (yesterday/last weekend).
2. Ask _____ if he'd like to (go to the movies/have dinner) with you (tonight/the day after tomorrow).
3. Ask _____ if you should bring anything when you come to dinner at his house.
4. Suggest to _____ that you (go skiing/play chess) next weekend.
5. Invite _____ to your house for dinner.
6. Accept an invitation.
7. Turn down an invitation. Give a reason.
8. Describe a nice way to spend an evening.

11. Talking on the Telephone

A. Taking Messages

1. You have dialed a number. Say "hello" and ask whoever answers if _____ is there.

2. Ask the person when _____ will be back.

3. Ask the person if you can leave a message.

4. Tell the person that it is important that _____ call you.

5. Tell the person to have _____ call you (at home/at work).

6. You have just answered the phone. Say "hello." Tell the caller that the person he wants isn't in.

7. Ask the caller who you should say called.

8. Give the message you have taken on the phone to _____ . Tell him who called and why.

B. Getting Information

1. Tell the operator you're having trouble calling a number.

2. Ask the operator if he can give you the number of Joe's Garage on Main Street.

3. Tell the operator you need a listing for _____ . Give his address.

4. Ask the operator if he said "2334" or "2344".

5. You want the telephone number of _____ so you call information. Give the operator the information he needs.

C. Long Distance Calls

1. Tell the operator you'd like to place a call to (Tehran/Abidjan).

2. Tell the operator you'd like to book a call to (Hong Kong/Rome).

3. Give the operator your area code and telephone number.

4. Tell the operator your call is person-to-person, not station-to-station.

5. You're at a pay phone. Dial the operator. Ask him how much it will cost to make a call to (Dallas/Milwaukee).

D. Unwanted Calls

1. Tell the caller he has the wrong number.

2. Ask the caller what number he's dialing.

3. Tell the caller he'd better check the listing again.

4. A telephone salesman calls you. Tell him you're not interested in his product.

5. You have just received the third call in one week from a company which sells vacuum cleaners. You're tired of this situation. Tell the salesman that you'd love to buy his product. Give the salesman the wrong address.

6. You wanted to call a friend and you have dialed the wrong number. Apologize.

12. Making Excuses

1. Give _____ a reason for not calling him last night.

2. Tell _____ why you couldn't come to a party.

3. Ask _____ if you were supposed to (call him/pick him up) last night.

4. Tell _____ that you were late because you (had a flat tire/were in a traffic jam).

5. Tell _____ you can't accept his invitation because you (already have other plans/are leaving town).

6. Yesterday you accepted an invitation, but today you want to cancel it. Offer an excuse.

7. Turn down an invitation to dinner.

8. You don't feel like going to work. Call your place of work. Give an excuse for not coming to work.

APPENDIX ONE
Answers to Presentation Lesson Exercises

Lesson 1

Part A:
Exercise A: short, long, short, long, short
Part B:
Exercise A: short, long, long, short, long
Part C:
Exercise A: and, or, and, or, or, and, or, and, and, or

Lesson 2

Exercise B: a, the, the, the, the, X, a, a, a, a, a, a, a, the, a, a, the, X, the, the

Lesson 3

Part A:
Exercise A: short, short, long, short, long
Exercise B: used to, hopes to, wants to, to Bob, ought to . . . to class, has to, need to, are going to, to talk to, to Jack

Part B:
Exercise A: short, long, long, long, short
Exercise B: for me, for him, for an hour, for a good book, for a while, for me, for an hour, for $7.98, for long, for the bus

Part C:
Exercise A: short, short, long, short, short
Exercise B: of yours, of the year, of the time, of the, of the tapes, of the paper, of minutes, of mistakes, of the building, out of order

Lesson 4

Exercise A: She's, He's, I'm, She's, He's, It's, We're, He's, They're, It's

Lesson 5

Exercise A: Who's, There's, Bob's, What's, What's, Here's, The letter's, Where's, Bill's, There's

Lesson 6

Exercise A: There'll, I'll, It'll, She'll, Mike'll, There'll You'll, He'll, They'll, The doctor'll

Lesson 7

Exercise A: I've, They've, She's, Bill's, We've, It's, He's, She's, I've, I've

Lesson 8

Exercise A: We'd like, I'd like, We'd like, We'd be, You'd have, I'd offer, It'd be, I'd like an, She'd like, you'd enjoy

Lesson 9

Exercise A: we'd better, You'd better, I'd better, We'd already seen, You'd better, I'd already gone, he'd better rest, We'd better call, You'd better call, he'd forgotten

Lesson 10

Exercise A: wasn't, haven't, isn't, aren't, shouldn't, hasn't, didn't, can't, won't, won't, hadn't, aren't, aren't, doesn't, don't, won't, doesn't, weren't, couldn't, shouldn't

Lesson 11

Exercise A: isn't, isn't, wasn't, isn't, wasn't, isn't, wasn't, isn't, isn't, wasn't isn't

Lesson 12

Exercise A: aren't, weren't, aren't, aren't, weren't, aren't, aren't, aren't, weren't, weren't

Lesson 13

Exercise A: short, long, short, long, short
Exercise B: here, her, her, his, her her, here, him, his, her, him

Lesson 14

Part B:
Exercise A: them, them, him, him, him, him, them, of them, him, of them, of them

Lesson 15

Exercise A: short, long, long, short, long
Exercise B: is going, is living, is borrowing, am trying, is reading, are being, is trying, are you doing, being, have been living

Lesson 16

Exercise A: short, short, short, short, long

Exercise B: want to, are going to, have to, Is he going to, Do we have to, Do you want to see, You have to mail, He's going to, They're not going to, She's going to

Lesson 17

Exercise A: short, long, short, long, short, short, short, long, short, long

Exercise B: Am I, Is that, Is she, Is it, Is this, Is there, Is it, Is he, Are they, Are we

Lesson 18

Exercise A: short, short, long, long, long

Exercise B: Was that, Was there, Were you, Was I, Were you, Was it, Was that, Was I, Were those, Were you

Lesson 19

Exercise A: Are you, Was it, Is she, Is there, Were you, Is he, Is this, Was that, Were they, Are these, Was there, Is she, Were you, Was he, Is this

Lesson 20

Exercise A: short, long, long, short, long, short, short

Exercise B: What are you, Why are they, When are we, What are you going, When are they, When are you, What's going to, Where are they, How are we, What is that, Where is it, What is he, How is she, When is he, What's the

Lesson 21

Exercise A: long, long, short, short, long

Exercise B: Who was she, Why was he, What were they, When were you, Where was I, Why were you, When was she, Where were, How was it, Who were you, Where was I, How were we, talking When was it, What were you doing

Lesson 22

Exercise A: What are you, How is he, When is it, Why were you, What's he, Why are they, Why were they, Who is she, When were you, How far is it, When is the, How much was it, When is she, Why is she speaking, What were you doing

Lesson 23

Exercise A: long, short, short, long, short

Exercise B: don't, doesn't, doesn't, didn't, doesn't, don't, don't, doesn't live, don't have, doesn't snow

Lesson 24

Exercise A: long, short, long, short, long

Exercise B: Does he, Do you, Do we, Does she, Do they, Do we have to leave, Do they live, Does that, Do they work, Does he

Lesson 25

Exercise A: long, short, short, long, short

Exercise B: Did she, Did he, Did we, Did they, Did you, Did you, Did she, Did you go, Did he come, Did that

Lesson 26

Exercise A: Does she, Do you, Do they, Does it, Do I, Does he, Did I, Did he, Did she, Did we, Did they, Did you, Did they, Do you, Do you, Does he, Does she, Do you, Do we, Do they

Exercise B: Do you speak, Does she live, Did he give you, Did you remember, Did you go, Did you understand, Does she visit, Do we, Do you take, Did it rain

Lesson 27

Exercise A: short, short, long, short, short

Exercise B: Why does it, Where do you, How long does it, How do you, What does he, How much does it, Where do you do, How do they like, What does she have, When do you have

Lesson 28

Exercise A: long, long, short, long, long

Exercise B: What did you, Where did they, When did you, What did she, Who did he, Where did they hear, Why did she ask, When did it open, Where did you buy, When did you come to the United States?

Lesson 29

Exercise A: Why does that, How do you, Where did you, When did they, What did you, How much does it, Where did you, What did she, When did they, How long does it, When did you, Why do you, How do you, When does he, What did she, Why did it, How did he, How did you, Who did he, Where did that

Exercise B: When did it begin, How do you want, Who do I have, Why did he miss, What did she say

Lesson 30

Exercise A: Aren't you, Isn't it, She's . . . isn't she, Isn't he, Weren't you, Aren't there, He's . . . isn't he, Aren't we, Aren't they, Wasn't it

Lesson 31

Exercise A: short, short, short, long, long

Exercise B: Doesn't she, Didn't you, Don't you, Didn't you, Doesn't he, Didn't you, Doesn't he, Don't you, Don't they, Don't you, didn't it, didn't she, don't you, didn't he, didn't she

Lesson 32

Exercise A: long, short, short, long, long

Exercise B: Have you, Has he, Has she, Have you ever, Have you, Have they done, Have there been, Has he solved, Have you heard, Has it started to rain

Lesson 33

Exercise A: short, short, long, long, short

Exercise B: We have, I have, He has, She has, They have, I have, They have, You have, he has, We have

Lesson 34

Exercise A: short, long, short, long, short

Exercise B: Can you, Could you, Can I, Will you, Can that, Will he, Should I, Can we get, Should we Come, would you do

Lesson 35

Exercise A: short, short, short, long, short

Exercise B: I shouldn't have, He must have, I could have, He could have, That couldn't have, I wouldn't have thought, might have mixed up, will have stopped, We would have eaten, It could have been

APPENDIX TWO
Complete Dialogs

1. Getting There

A. At the Airport

1. *Customer:* When do you have flights for Las Vegas on Saturday?
   Agent: We have flights at 9:30 a.m. and 3:40 p.m.
   Customer: When do they arrive in Las Vegas?
   Agent: 10:30 a.m. and 4:40 p.m.
   Customer: How much is the fare?
   Agent: One way is $22.50 plus tax. Round trip is $38.75.

2. *Agent:* How do you want to fly: coach or first class?
   Customer: Coach is cheaper, isn't it?
   Agent: Yes, coach fare is more economical.
   Customer: I think I'll fly coach on the 9:30 a.m. flight.

3. *Agent:* Here you go, ma'am. This is your boarding pass.
   Customer: Where's the departure gate?
   Agent: Gate 10. It's straight ahead past the security check area.

4. *Customer:* Which gate does my plane leave from?
   Agent: It leaves from Gate 22.
   Customer: Is that this way or that way?
   Agent: It's to your left. You'd better hurry. They're loading right now.

5. *Woman:* Excuse me. Is the five-thirty flight from Denver on time?
   Agent: No, ma'am. It's been delayed.
   Woman: Delayed? For how long?
   Agent: For at least an hour. There's been a bad snow storm in Denver.

B. Buses, Local and Long Distance

6. *Passenger:* Excuse me, driver. Does this bus go past the university?

   Driver: No, not this bus. You'll have to transfer downtown.

   Passenger: Which bus do I take from there?

   Driver: I believe it's the number four bus.

7. *Passenger:* Will this bus take me to MacArthur Park?

   Driver: Nope. You've got to transfer at Central Avenue.

   Passenger: Which bus should I take?

   Driver: All of the Central Avenue buses go past the park.

8. *Passenger:* This bus goes past the university, doesn't it?

   Driver: It goes near the university.

   Passenger: When should I get off?

   Driver: Get off at Fourth Street and walk two blocks east.

9. *Passenger:* This bus will take me to the Capitol Building, won't it?

   Driver: Yep. It sure will.

   Passenger: How much is the fare?

   Driver: Fifty cents. Exact change.

   Passenger: Here you are.

   Driver: Don't give it to me. Drop it in the box.

10. *Customer:* How much is the fare to San Francisco via Los Angeles?

    Agent: It's $55.

    Customer: Can I get off in L.A. for a few days?

    Agent: Sure. Your ticket is good for three weeks.

11. *Man:* When will the bus stop for lunch?

    Woman: I think the driver said we'd stop at 12:30.

    Man: How long will we have to eat?

    Woman: The lunch stop is for an hour.

C. Taxis

12.   *Man:* Red Cab Taxi Company. Can I help you?

   Woman: Please send a taxi to the Hilton Hotel.

   Man: What's your name?

   Woman: Alice Jones.

   Man: A cab will be there in ten minutes.

13. *Passenger:* Is this taxi taken?

   Driver: No. Where are you going?

   Passenger: To the Lincoln Park Apartments. They're on 44th Street.

   Driver: I know where they are. Get in.

14.   *Driver:* Which terminal are you going to?

   Passenger: Japan Air Lines.

   Driver: Here you are, sir.

   Passenger: Fine. How much is the fare?

   Driver: Six-forty.

   Passenger: Here's seven dollars. Keep the change.

D. Renting a Car

15. *Customer:* Is it possible to rent a car from here?

   Agent: Yes. Did you call in advance?

   Customer: No, I didn't. I've just arrived in town.

   Agent: Well, all that we have available right now is a Nova.

   Customer: That'll be fine. How much is it per day?

   Agent: Twenty dollars per day. There's no limit on mileage.

16. *Customer:* I'd like to rent a car for the day.

   Agent: Fine, sir. We have Pintos, Granadas, and Mercuries.

   Customer: Let's see. Which is the cheapest? The Pinto?

   Agent: That's right. It's ten dollars a day, plus ten cents a mile.

17   *Agent:* How long do you need the car for?

   Customer: Three days at most.

   Agent: I need to see your driver's license and a major credit card.

   Customer: Here's my bank credit card. Will that do?

   Agent: That's fine.

E. Getting Directions

18.   *Woman:* Do you know how to get to Paul's house from here?

            Man: Yeh. Stay on this road until you get to Glenn Road. Then take a left.

       Woman: Left on Glenn Road, OK . . . .

            Man: Stay on Glenn Road for about four blocks until you come to Washington Street. Then turn right.

       Woman: Left on Glenn, right on Washington, ...

            Man: He lives at 222 Washington. It's on the right side of the street.

19.   *Man:* Should I turn right here?

       Woman: No. Keep going straight and turn at the next light.

            Man: Do you mean at Scott Road?

       Woman: That's right. Turn right there.

20.   *Man:* How far is it from here to L.A.?

       Woman: Oh, about seven hours by car.

            Man: What's the best way to get there?

       Woman: I-10 is the fastest.

2. As Time Goes By

A. Making Appointments

21.   *Man:* I'd like to make an appointment to see Dr. Taylor.

  Receptionist: OK. Let's see. He's available on Tuesday or Thursday.

            Man: Thursday would be better for me.

  Receptionist: Morning or afternoon?

            Man: In the morning, if possible.

  Receptionist: How does 9:15 sound?

            Man: 9:15 Thursday. That's fine.

22.   *Man:* What time will the doctor be in today?

  Receptionist: He's here after 2:30. Do you need to see him today?

            Man: Yes. My back's killing me.

  Receptionist: The doctor's very busy, but I think we can fit you in at 5:15.

23.   *Man:*   I'm Mr. Wang. I have an appointment for 5:15.

    Receptionist: Please sign here. A nurse will call your name.

          Man: How long will it be before I can see the doctor?

    Receptionist: He'll be with you in a few minutes.

24.   *Receptionist:*   Your appointment isn't until 2:30.

          Man: I know. I'm here ahead of time.

25.   *Man:*   My tooth's bothering me. When can I see a doctor?

     Woman: How about tomorrow? 10:30 OK?

        Man: Isn't there anything earlier?

     Woman: No, but I'll call you if there's a cancellation before then.

26.   *Receptionist:*   Is this your first appointment with Dr. Dans?

          Man: Yes, it is. I'd like to have a dental check-up.

    Receptionist: Fill out this card and give it back to me.

          Man: All right. Do you have a pen?

27.   *Student:*   Would it be convenient to see you today?

    Professor: Yes. My office hours are 10:30 to noon.

      Student: I've been having trouble with the homework.

    Professor: Come by anytime. We'll talk about it.

28.   *Student:*   Is Doctor Harris in?

    Secretary: May I have your name?

      Student: Jack Stephens.

    Secretary: Let me check with her to tell her you're here.

29.   *Man:*   Ms. McGraw. This is Bill Sidelow from Acme Construction.

     Woman: Oh, hello, Mr. Sidelow, I'm glad you called. What can I do for you?

        Man: I'd like to drop by today to talk over your contract.

     Woman: Sure. How is one o'clock?

        Man: Can we make it a little later?

     Woman: Two-thirty, three?

        Man: Two-thirty would be great.

     Woman: Fine. I'll see you then.

B. Telling the Time

30.   *Man:*   What time do you have?

     Woman: I have a quarter to four.

     Man: Excuse me? What's the time?

     Woman: A quarter to four.

31.   *Woman:*   What time is it?

     Man: It's 8:15.

     Woman: Are you sure? My watch has 8:30.

     Man: Your watch must be fast.

32.   *Woman:*   Could you give me the time?

     Man: It's 9:05 exactly.

33.   *Man:*   What time have you got?

     Woman: About 7:30.

34.   *Man:*   Can you tell me what time it is?

     Woman: I'm sorry. I don't have a watch.

35.   *Man:*   Can that clock be right? 10:30?

     Woman: That clock is always off. It's 11:05.

36.   *Woman:*   Check the time. There's a clock in the kitchen.

     Man: It's a little before nine.

37.   *Woman:*   Are we going to be late?

     Man: We will be unless we hurry.

     Woman: When does the show start?

     Man: At eight-thirty. We've got fifteen minutes to get there.

38.   *Man:*   Do we have time to grab a quick bite?

     Woman: We've got thirty minutes before the meeting. Let's go eat.

39.   *Man:*   Come on. Let's go. The plane leaves in ten minutes.

     Woman: Let's hurry. We've got just enough time to make it.

40.   *Man:*   Do you have the time?

      Woman: It's about three-thirty.

      Man: Oh, no. I'm late. I have an appointment in fifteen minutes.

      Woman: Don't worry. I'll drive you wherever you have to go.

41.   *Man:*   How long did you spend on that report?

      Woman: I spent several hours on it.

42.   *Man:*   Did you spend much time in Europe?

      Woman: Oh, yes. I was there for four months.

43.   *Woman:*   Did it take much time to get your passport?

      Man: No. It took about ten days.

3.   Getting Along With People

A. Meeting and Greeting

44.   *Woman:*   Hi, Bill.

      Man: Hi, Jill. How are you?

      Woman: Fine, thanks. You?

      Man: All right.

45.   *Man:*   Hi Margaret. How are you doing?

      Woman: Really fine. How about yourself?

      Man: Could be better, but not bad.

      Woman: Mmm. That's good.

46.   *Man-1:*   Well, it seems as if you're new here.

      Man-2:   Yes. My family and I have just moved to Phoenix.

      Man-1:   What type of business are you in?

      Man-2:   I run a management consulting firm.

47.   *Woman:* Have you been in Houston long?

       Man: Two years, more or less.

     Woman: How do you like it?

       Man: The people are friendly and the weather is nice.

B. Parting

48.   *Man:* I really hate to rush off like this.

   Woman: No problem. We know you're busy.

     Man: I want to get together again sometime soon.

49.   *Woman:* I really have to be going.

    Man: Stay! Stay a little while longer.

  Woman: No. You've been too generous.

    Man: Are you sure you have to go?

  Woman: Yes. It's really getting late.

50.   *Man-1:* It's ten o'clock. I'm going to have to be leaving.

  Man-2: Leaving? Already?

  Man-1: Yes. I've got to get up early tomorrow.

  Man-2: OK. Stop over again sometime.

51.   *Man:* Excuse me, Mary. I have to take off.

 Woman: OK. But wouldn't you like to have another drink?

   Man: No, I'd really better not.

 Woman: All right. I'll see you later. Take care of yourself.

C. Gossiping

52.   *Man:* Did you hear what happened to Margo?

 Woman: No, but I'm dying to hear the story.

   Man: She and her boss had an argument.

 Woman: Where did you hear that?

   Man: Someone in her office told me.

53. **Woman:** Have you heard the latest?

 Man: No. What's the latest?

 Woman: Mrs. Bender's being fired.

 Man: What did she do?

 Woman: It's not what she did; it's what she didn't do. She forgot to enter $25,000 in the company records.

 Man: Don't you think her boss will forgive her?

 Woman: Not this time. It's happened before.

54. **Woman:** Well, wouldn't you know it?

 Man: Know what? Aren't you going to tell me?

 Woman: Jackie has quit her job, according to the newspaper.

 Man: Why was she working anyway? She's rich.

 Woman: She wanted something to do, I guess.

 Man: With all that money, she ought to have people working for her.

55. **Man-1:** Do you want to hear something interesting?

 Man-2: Yeh. What?

 Man-1: Did you know that Tom Kelly used to work in a zoo?

 Man-2: No, you're kidding. How do you know that?

 Man-1: Oh, he told me about it the other day.

56. **Woman:** Do you think John and Jill are going to get married?

 Man: I don't know. Do you think they are?

 Woman: Sure. Don't you see them together all the time?

D. Talking about the Weather

57. **Woman:** What is it like outside today?

 Man: It's clear and sunny but cold.

 Woman: I'd better wear my heavy jacket.

 Man: That's a good idea.

117

58.　　　　Man:　Do you think it's going to rain today?

　　　Woman:　I don't know. I hope so.

　　　　Man:　You want it to rain?

　　　Woman:　Yes. It's been so dry lately.

59.　　　　Man:　Boy, it's really a nice day today, isn't it?

　　　Woman:　It is. Looks like spring is coming soon.

　　　　Man:　Yeh. It'll just be a few more weeks.

60.　　　Woman:　When is it going to stop raining?

　　　　Man:　I don't know. It should have stopped by now.

　　　Woman:　If this keeps up, we'll have to get a boat.

　　　　Man:　Oh, well. I've always enjoyed fishing.

4.　Buying Things

A.　Getting Information

61.　　　　Man:　What time do these stores close?

　　　Woman:　Most of them close at six.

　　　　Man:　How about Aron's Music Shop?

　　　Woman:　I think that's open until nine.

62.　　Woman-1　Where do you do your shopping?

　　　Woman-2:　Do you mean clothes shopping or food shopping?

　　　Woman-1:　Your clothes shopping.

　　　Woman-2:　I generally go to Damond's Department Store.

63.　　　Man-1:　Where did you buy that sweater?

　　　　Man-2:　I bought it at Damond's Department Store.

　　　　Man-1:　How much did it cost?

　　　　Man-2:　It was twenty-three dollars or something like that.

64.   *Salesman:* Do you need any help?

           Man: Yes. I'm looking for pants.

    Salesman: What's your size?

           Man: Thirty waist and thirty-six inseam.

65.   *Woman:* Excuse me. Could you help me?

  Saleswoman: Certainly. What do you need?

     Woman: I'm looking for a blouse, size 10.

  Saleswoman: There are several over here. Could you come this way?

66.   *Man:* Pardon me. Where are the dressing rooms?

  Saleswoman: There's one next to the suit rack.

       Man: Can you hold these packages for me?

  Saleswoman: No, but I'll put them behind the cash register. They'll be safe.

67.   *Woman:* Where do you keep the ice cream?

      Clerk: It's in the frozen food section.

    Woman: Where's that?

      Clerk: It's two aisles to the left of the center of the store.

68.   *Man:* I can't find the instant soup.

    Clerk: Did you look next to the canned soup?

      Man: I looked there, but there isn't any on the shelf.

    Clerk: Why don't you try the spice section. It ought to be there.

69.   *Man:* Can you tell me where I can find the butter?

    Clerk: Yes. It's with dairy goods in the back of the store.

70.   *Woman:* Excuse me. I can't find the canned fruit.

    Clerk: It's in aisle nine next to the fruit juices.

B. Asking Prices

71.   *Man:* How much does this book cost? It doesn't have a price on it.

        Clerk: That book is four ninety-five. The price is on the inside cover.

72.   *Woman:* How much do these cost?

        Clerk: They're $17.98.

        Woman: Don't you think that's expensive for a pair of gloves?

        Clerk: Not at all. That's the best price in town.

73.   *Woman:* What's the price of these gloves?

        Clerk: They're on sale for $18.98.

        Woman: On sale? Broadway has the same pair for $17.98.

        Clerk: Let me look again. Oh, yes. They're $8.98.

C. Paying for It

74.   *Man:* Where do I pay for this shirt?

    Salesperson: You'd better take it to the next register.

        Man: Can't I pay for it here?

    Salesperson: You could have a few minutes ago, but I've closed out for the night.

75.   *Clerk:* Do you want to pay for it with cash or with a check?

        Woman: Is it possible to use a credit card?

        Clerk: No, we don't accept credit cards in this store.

76.   *Clerk:* That's twenty-nine on the bananas, fifty-three on the juice, one twenty-nine on the chicken, and eighty-nine on the milk. . . Will there be anything else?

        Man: No, that's all.

        Clerk: That's three dollars even, plus fifteen tax. . . . three fifteen.

        Man: Here's five. . . . and the fifteen in change.

77.   *Salesman:* So would you like this clock radio?
      Man: Yes. I'll take it.
      Salesman: Will this be cash or charge?
      Man: I have a Mastercharge card.

D.   Returning Items

78.   *Woman:* Do you suppose I can return these gloves?
      Saleswoman: What's the matter with them?
      Woman: They're the wrong size.
      Saleswoman: Didn't you try them on before you bought them?
      Woman: I didn't have time. The store was closing.

79.   *Woman:* Could I return these gloves?
      Salesperson: Did you buy them on sale?
      Woman: Yes, but they're too small.
      Salesperson: I'm sorry. Sales on sale items are final.
      Woman: Let me talk to the manager.
      Salesperson: I am the manager, ma'am.

80.   *Woman:* Pardon me. I received these gloves as a gift. They're too small.
      Salesman: Did they come from this Broadway store?
      Woman: I'm pretty sure. Don't you sell this item?
      Salesman: Yes, we do. We can't give you a cash return, but we can give you a credit voucher.
      Woman: That would be fine. I think you sell these gloves for $17.98.
      Salesman: That's right. Here's your voucher. It's good for $17.98 on any store purchase.

81.   *Man:* I'd like to return this radio?
      Salesperson: What seems to be the problem?
      Man: The dial is broken. It doesn't turn.
      Salesperson: We can replace it for you. Do you have your receipt?

82.   *Woman:*   I'd like to return this record. It has a scratch on it.

    Salesperson: I'm sorry. We can't refund or replace records.

       Woman: But there's a scratch on it.

    Salesperson: I'm sorry. That's the store policy.

5. Eating and Drinking

A. Arriving

83.   *Man:*   We've got reservations for a party of six.

    Woman: What's your name?

      Man: My name is George McClintock.

    Woman: Yes, sir. If you'll come this way, I'll show you to your table.

84.   *Man:*   I'd like to make reservations for 8:00 tonight.

    Woman: How many will be in your group?

      Man: There'll be two of us.

    Woman: And the name of the party please?

      Man: Hill.

    Woman: That's Hill, party of two, 8:00 Saturday.

85.   *Woman:*   Good evening. How many are there in your party?

      Man: There're four of us.

    Woman: And what's your name please?

      Man: Bryant. B-R-Y-A-N-T.

    Woman: Ok, Mr. Bryant. There'll be a short wait. If you'd like to wait in the lounge, we'll give you a call.

B. Ordering

86.   *Hostess:*   Good evening. Are you here for dinner or just cocktails.

      Man: We're here just for drinks.

    Hostess: Fine. The cocktail lounge is to your right.

87.   *Man:* Waiter, do you have a bar list?

   Waiter: Yes, here you are. What would you like this evening?

   Man: What's the bar special?

   Waiter: Tonight, it's double scotch on the rocks.

88.   *Woman:* What do you want to drink, sir?

   Man: Make that a gin and tonic.

   Woman: Could I get you anything else?

   Man: Yes, could you bring us some nuts.

89.   *Man:* Bartender, can you give me a draft beer?

   Bartender: Sure. We have Bud and Coors on tap.

   Man: I'll have a Bud.

90.   *Woman:* Waiter, we'd like to order now.

   Waiter: Yes? What would you like to begin with?

   Woman: Which salad do you recommend?

   Waiter: I'd suggest the Chef's delight.

   Woman: Does it have cheese in it?

   Waiter: Yes, it does. It's always been a favorite with our customers.

91.   *Waitress:* May I take your order please?

   Man: Yes, I'd like the prime rib dinner.

   Waitress: That comes with potatoes. Would you like a baked potato or french fries?

   Man: Baked potato.

   Waitress: And what kind of dressing would you like on your salad?

   Man: What kinds have you got?

   Waitress: Italian, French, and Blue Cheese.

   Man: I'll have Italian.

92.   *Waitress:* How's your dinner, sir?

   Man: It's just fine.

   Waitress: Can I bring you anything?

   Man: No, thanks. Everything's fine.

93.   *Woman:* I think we'll just have coffee.

        Waitress: Wouldn't you like anything else?

        Woman: No, that'll be all. Thank you.

        Waitress: Here's your check.

94.   *Man:* Can you bring us our check, please?

        Waitress: Yes, sir. Right away.

C. Problems with the Food

95.   *Man:* Waiter, this steak should have been cooked longer.

        Waiter: How did you order it?

        Man: Medium rare, but this is practically raw!

        Waiter: Well, I'll return it and bring you another.

96.   *Waitress:* Yes, is there something wrong?

        Man: I think you've made a mistake. This isn't what I ordered.

        Waitress: I'm sorry. I must have confused orders.

97.   *Woman:* Waiter, can you come here for a second please?

        Waiter: What's the problem, ma'am?

        Woman: This soup is cold.

        Waiter: I'm sorry. I'll bring you a hot one.

D. Fast Food

98.   *Woman:* Next. May I help you?

        Man: Yeh. I want a superburger, fries, and a large coke.

        Woman: Super, fries, large coke. That'll be a dollar twenty-seven.

99.
  Man: Who's next?

 Woman: I want an order of french fries and a small coke.

  Man: Anything else?

 Woman: No, that's all.

  Man: How about a hamburger or an apple pie?

 Woman: No, just french fries and a small coke?

  Man: OK. That's fifty-nine cents.

100.
 Woman: Yes, sir. What'll it be for you?

  Man: Two hamburgers and french fries.

 Woman: Is there anything else?

  Man: No, that's it.

 Woman: Is this to go or to eat here?

  Man: We'll be eating here.

101.
  Man: Don't you have any ketchup?

 Woman: It's on the service counter.

  Man: Where do you keep the salt and pepper?

 Woman: You'll find it in the same place.

6. Talking at School

A. In the Classroom

102.
 Student: I don't know this word.

 Teacher: Do you mean "apricot"?

 Student: Yes. How do you say it in Spanish?

 Teacher: I don't know. I don't speak Spanish.

103.
 Student-1: How do you say "mañana" in English?

 Student-2: I think the word is "tomorrow" in English.

104.
 Student: What's the meaning of this word?

 Teacher: What word are you talking about?

 Student: I want to know the meaning of this word "split."

 Teacher: It means "to divide."

105. *Student-1:* How would you translate this sentence into Chinese?

      Student-2: What's the sentence?

      Student-1: "The more, the merrier."

      Student-2: I have no idea.

106. *Student:* Could you repeat that answer again please?

      Teacher: Yes. The correct answer is "B".

      Student: Did you say "B" or "D"?

      Teacher: "B" as in "boy."

107. *Student:* Can you help me with this problem?

      Teacher: What's the problem?

      Student: I haven't had much math and this problem requires trigonometry.

      Teacher: Let's see. That's not too difficult. Let me give you a hand.

108. *Student-1:* I don't like our new teacher. Do you?

      Student-2: Oh, he's not too bad. I've had worse teachers.

      Student-1: Doesn't he give us too much homework?

      Student-2: Yeh. He does give us a lot.

109. *Student-1:* This class is awfully big, isn't it?

      Student-2: Yeh. There are too many students.

      Student-1: I should have signed up for a different class.

      Student-2: Right. You can learn more in smaller classes.

110. *Student-1:* Hey, John. Were you in the lab yesterday?

      Student-2: No, I couldn't make it. Weren't you there either?

      Student-1: No, I wasn't. Darn. I was hoping you could tell me the assignment.

      Student-2: I guess we'll have to get it from somebody else.

111. *Student:* Where's the best place to buy a good dictionary?

      Teacher: Have you tried the campus bookstore?

      Student: Yes. But the ones there are not English-English dictionaries.

      Teacher: Then, try to get one at Blue and Gray Bookstore.

7. Apartment Living

A. Finding a Place to Live

112.   *Woman:* Excuse me. Do you have any vancancies?

              Man: No, we don't. Didn't you see the sign out front?

        Woman: No, I didn't see a sign.

              Man: Well, we won't have any vacancies until May 1.

113.   *Man:* I'm calling about the ad for the apartment.

      Woman: The apartment's still available.

          Man: How much is the rent?

      Woman: It's $170 per month.

          Man: That include utilities?

      Woman: Yes, they're included.

114.   *Woman:* Do I have to sign a lease for this apartment?

          Man: No, you don't, but there'll be a deposit.

    Woman: Is the deposit refundable?

          Man: Oh, yes. You'll get it back when you leave.

115.   *Woman:* Are all of your apartments two-bedroom apartments?

          Man: No. We also have one-bedroom and studio apartments.

    Woman: What's the difference in price?

          Man: Two bedrooms are two thirty, one-bedrooms are two ten, and studios are one eighty.

116.   *Man:* Did you sign a lease on your apartment?

    Woman: Yes, our landlord has given us a year's lease.

        Man: Do you like your new place?

    Woman: Yes, it's got all the modern conveniences.

B. Getting a Phone

117.   *Woman:* Hello. My name is Mary Alvero. I'd like to have a phone put in my new apartment.

        Man: What's the address of your apartment, Miss Alvero?

    Woman: 1107 East Alto Avenue, Apartment 5.

        Man: We'll send someone out a week from Thursday.

118.   *Man:* I'd like to have a phone installed in my home.

    Woman: Do you make many long distance calls?

      Man: Yes, we do. We make quite a few.

    Woman: Then we'll have to ask for a large deposit.

119.   *Man:* South Central Bell. May I help you?

    Woman: Yes, I'd like you to install a phone in my apartment.

      Man: Have you had previous service with us?

    Woman: No, I haven't. I'm new here.

120.   *Woman:* Do I need to put down a deposit?

      Man: Yes, it'll be $50. It's refundable.

    Woman: Where do I put down the deposit?

      Man: You'll have to come to our office on Main Street.

C. Problems

121.   *Woman:* Excuse me. I hate to disturb you, but . . . .

      Man: You're the new tenant in twelve-B, aren't you?

    Woman: That's right. I'm having a problem with the toilet.

               It won't stop flushing.

      Man: OK. Just a minute. I'll come up and take a look.

122. **Woman:** Hi. Here's the check for this month's rent.

     Man: Wait a minute. I'll give you a receipt.

     By the way, are you having any problems in your apartment?

     Woman: Well, as a matter of fact, the heater doesn't work too well, and the garbage disposal is broken.

     Man: Hmmm. I'll try to look into those things sometime this week.

123. **Woman:** Oh, no! Not again!

     Man: What's wrong? Is there something the matter with the sink?

     Woman: Yes, it's gotten stopped up again.

     Man: I guess we'd better call a plumber.

124. **Woman 1:** The landlord wants to raise my rent again.

     Woman 2: Did you ask him why?

     Woman 1: He says that it's because of inflation.

     Woman 2: Well, I'd talk to the housing authorities if I were you.

8. Taking Care of Business

A. At the Post Office

125. **Woman:** I want to mail this letter overseas.

     Clerk: That's 31¢ per half ounce for overseas mail.

     Woman: That's expensive. How much are aerograms?

     Clerk: They're twenty-two cents a piece.

126. **Man:** How long does it take for a letter to get to Iran?

     Clerk: It'll take five or six days.

     Man: I want to register it.

     Clerk: All right. It'll probably take a little longer to get there though.

127.   *Woman:* Is it possible to get a post office box?

        Clerk: Certainly. Fill out this form.

    Woman: How much is the rent?

        Clerk: It's twenty dollars per year.

128.   *Clerk:* Next, please. I can help you down here.

    Woman: I'd like four aerograms and three thirteen-cent stamps.

        Clerk: Did you say three aerograms and four stamps?

    Woman: No, the other way around.

B. At the Bank

129.   *Man:* I'd like to open a savings and a checking account.

    Woman: Our minimum deposit for a savings account is $25.

      Man: What is the interest rate?

    Woman: It's 4 1/2%.

      Man: Do you charge for checks?

    Woman: Each check that you write will cost 20¢.

130.   *Woman:* I'd like to withdraw some money from my savings account.

    Teller: First you'll have to fill out one of these withdrawal forms.

   Woman: Oh, no. It asks for my account number. I forgot my bank book.

    Teller: I'm afraid you'll need that first.

131.   *Man:* Can I cash a check here?

    Teller: Do you have an account with us?

     Man: Yes, I have a checking account here.

    Teller: Please write your account number on the back of the check.

     Man: Is that all you need?

    Teller: Could I see one more piece of identification?

     Man: Will a driver's license do?

    Teller: Yes. That'd be fine.

132.   *Man:* I would like to ask about taking out a loan.

Loan Officer: Do you have an account here?

Man: Yes, I've been a customer here for several months.

Loan Officer: How much do you want to borrow?

Man: Three thousand dollars.

C. Auto Repair

133.   *Attendant:* Yes, sir. May I help you?

Man: Could you fill it up with regular?

Attendant: Sure. Do you want me to check the oil and water?

Man: If you would please.

134.   *Woman:* Could you check my battery?

Attendant: What's the problem?

Woman: The car is hard to start.

Attendant: Hmm. The battery seems OK. Maybe something else is wrong.

135.   *Man:* Is there anything wrong with the car?

Attendant: Not really. You just need a tune-up.

Man: Is that going to be expensive?

Attendant: It'll cost $23.50.

Man: When can you get to it?

Attendant: If you leave the car now, I can finish it by five today.

136.   *Woman:* Have you found out what the problem is?

Mechanic: Yep. You need a new carburetor and fuel pump.

Woman: You have to replace both of them?

Mechanic: Absolutely. There's no other way.

Woman: I think I'll get a second opinion.

D. Immigration

137. *Immigration Officer:* How long do you plan to be in the United States?

      Woman: Just a couple of months.

      Immigration Officer: What's your reason for wanting to go?

      Woman: I'm going as a tourist.

      Immigration Officer: Do you have any relatives in the U.S.?

      Woman: Yes. My son's a student at the University of California.

138. *Officer:* What kind of visa do you have?

      Man: It's a student visa.

      Officer: When did you enter the United States?

      Man: I came into the country on August 6th.

      Officer: What was your port of entry?

      Man: New York City, Kennedy Airport.

139. *Officer:* Mister VanHoff. We understand that you're not attending school.

      Man: No, I've been attending, but I've been sick recently.

      Officer: You've attended only three days since last July.

      Man: Three days? No, it's been more than that.

      Officer: We're going to have to take away your visa.

140. *Officer:* Number forty-six?

      Woman: That's me. I have a problem. I've lost my visa.

      Officer: You'll have to see Miss Vance. She'll be back at two.

      Woman: But I've been waiting here all morning.

141. *Man:* I would like to extend my visa.

      Officer: Are you on a tourist visa or a student visa?

      Man: It's an F-1 visa.

      Officer: We'll need a letter from your school and a financial statement from you.

E. At the Doctor's Office

142.   *Nurse:* The doctor will see you now. Come this way.

        Man: Where's the examination room?

        Nurse: It's to your right. You can lie down on the table.

143.   *Doctor:* What seems to be the problem, Mrs. Allen?

        Woman: I've been having pains in my chest recently.

        Doctor: Do you have difficulty breathing.

        Woman: Sometimes. But not too much.

        Doctor: Well, let's take an X-Ray of your chest.

144.   *Doctor:* Here's a prescription. I'd like you to take one of these pills three times a day.

        Patient: Is there anything else I should do?

        Doctor: Yes. You should drink a lot of liquids and get a lot of rest.

        Patient: OK. Is there a pharmacy in this building?

        Doctor: No, but you can have that prescription filled at any drugstore.

145.   *Doctor:* You're suffering from an allergy.

        Patient: Is it serious?

        Doctor: No. I'll just give you a prescription.

        Patient: Where do I get the medicine?

        Doctor: There's a pharmacy in this building.

F. At the Barber Shop

146. *Customer:* I'd like to get a haircut, please.

        Barber: How do you want it cut?

    Customer: Don't cut it too short. Just trim it.

        Barber: Would you like me to shampoo your hair also?

    Customer: Yes. That'd be a good idea.

147. *Hairdresser:* How would you like your hair cut?

        Woman: It's getting a little too long, but don't cut it too much.

    Hairdresser: Do you want me to shape it?

        Woman: Yes, please do.

9. Staying at Hotels and Motels

148.   *Man:* I'd like a room for the night, please.

      Clerk: How many people are in your party?

       Man: There are two of us—my wife and myself.

      Clerk: We have a double for sixteen dollars.

149.   *Woman:* How much is a room for one night?

     Clerk: It's $14 for a single and $16 for a double.

   Woman: Does that include tax?

     Clerk: No, the tax is extra.

150.   *Clerk:* Did you call us in advance?

      Man: Yes. I made a reservation two weeks ago.

    Clerk: Well, I can't find your reservation card.

      Man: Would you please check again.

    Clerk: I'm sorry. I still can't find it.

151.   *Clerk:* What's your name, sir?

      Man: Albert Johnson. I called ahead two hours ago.

    Clerk: Oh, yes. Your room is 213. Here's your key.

      Man: Do I pay now or later?

    Clerk: You can pay when you check out.

152.   *Woman:* Do you have any vacancies?

     Clerk: I'm sorry, ma'am. We're completely booked.

   Woman: I should have made a reservation.

     Clerk: That would have helped.

153. **Man:** I have reservations for this weekend.

       Clerk: What is your name, sir?

       Man: Johnson. I called yesterday.

       Clerk: Yes. Here's your reservation card.

154. **Woman:** Where can I get something to eat?

       Clerk: There's a restaurant in the lobby.

       Woman: Do you bring food to the room?

       Clerk: Yes, we do. All you have to do is dial room service.

155. **Clerk:** Your room is 1456. It's on the fourteenth floor.

       Man: Does this place have an elevator?

       Clerk: It does, but it's being repaired right now.

156. **Man:** Have there been any messages for me—Mr. Jackson?

       Clerk: Let me check the box. No, there aren't any messages.

157. **Woman:** Does the hotel have a sauna?

       Clerk: Yes, there's a sauna and a steam room.

       Woman: Where are they located?

       Clerk: Both of them are through the lobby toward the pool area.

158. **Woman:** Is there a phone in the room?

       Clerk: All of our rooms have phones.

       Woman: Does it cost to make a call?

       Clerk: Yes. We charge 25¢ for each call.

159. **Man:** Is there a televsion in the room?

       Clerk: No, there isn't. Would you like one?

       Man: Yes, I would. How much is it per day?

       Clerk: It's two dollars a day extra.

160. **Woman:** Is there a public telephone here?

       Clerk: There's one across the lobby.

       Woman: I need to make a long distance call.

       Clerk: You can do that from your room. We'll add it to your bill.

161.   Clerk: Room Service. May I help you?
       Woman: Please send some toast and coffee up to Room 212.
       Clerk: Is that all, ma'am?
       Woman: Yes, that's all.

162.   Clerk: Good morning. Did you sleep well last night?
       Woman: Yes. The room was fine.
       Clerk: Are you checking out this morning?
       Woman: Yes, I'm leaving around ten.

163.   Clerk: How do you want to pay the bill?
       Man: Excuse me?
       Clerk: You can pay with cash or check or with a credit card.
       Man: I'll put it on my credit card.

164.   Woman: How can I get to the airport from here?
       Clerk: There's a bus from here to the airport every half hour.
       Woman: Is there a taxi stand nearby?
       Clerk: No, but I can call one for you.

10. Social Situations

A. Questions and Invitations

165.   Woman: What did you do last night?
       Man: I just stayed home.
       Woman: Didn't you go to the concert?
       Man: I was going to go, but then I decided not to.

166.   Man: Did you do anything over the weekend?
       Woman: Not much. What did you do?
       Man: I had planned to go skiing, but I wound up studying.

167. *Man-1:* What are you planning to do this weekend?

   Man-2: I have a lot of studying to do.

   Man-1: Aren't you going to go camping with us?

   Man-2: To tell you the truth, I really don't like to camp.

168. *Woman:* Mark, would you like to come over for dinner tomorrow night?

   Man: Oh, wow. That's nice. What time should I come by?

   Woman: Around seven or seven-thirty.

   Man: Great. Should I bring anything?

   Woman: You could bring a bottle of wine if you'd like.

169. *Man:* Would you like to join us for dinner tonight?

   Woman: I'd love to. What time should I come over?

   Man: We're planning dinner for eight o'clock.

   Woman: How should I dress?

   Man: This is informal. You can come as you are.

170. *Man:* Why don't you pay us a visit about nine tonight?

   Woman: What's the occasion?

   Man: It's Gloria's birthday and we're having a few friends over.

   Woman: Should I bring a gift?

   Man: Oh, no. It's a simple get-together.

171. *Man:* Let's take in a concert tonight.

   Woman: Good. I'd really like to hear some music.

   Man: And afterward we could go someplace quiet for a drink.

   Woman: That sounds like a nice way to spend the evening.

172. *Woman-1:* Hello.

   Woman-2: Jean, this is Ellen.

   Woman-1: Hi, Ellen. How are you?

   Woman-2: Fine. Say, I wonder if you'd like to catch a film with me tonight.

   Woman-1: What film are you planning to see?

   Woman-2: *The House of Horrors*—it's a thriller.

173. **Woman:** Hello.

Man: Hello, Jane. This is Pete. It's such a nice day today that I thought we might go to the zoo.

Woman: I wish you had called me earlier. I've just made plans to play tennis.

Man: Oh, that's too bad. Maybe some other time.

Woman: OK, Pete. Thanks for calling.

174. **Man:** How would you like to go out tonight?

Woman: Great. What did you have in mind?

Man: I thought we could see the new play at the university.

Woman: That sounds good. I hope we can get tickets.

175. **Man-1:** Hey, what are you doing this afternoon?

Man-2: Nothing special. Why?

Man-1: Let's get together for a beer or two.

176. **Man:** There's a street festival in Scottsdale this coming Saturday. Do you want to go?

Woman: Sure. Is it OK if we take your car?

Man: Fine. Why don't we leave around ten?

Woman: That's good. If we don't leave early, we won't get a parking space.

11. Talking on the Telephone

A. Taking Messages

177. **Woman:** Hello.

Man: Is Mary there, please?

Woman: No, she's out right now.

Man: When will she be back?

Woman: I'm not sure—probably around six. Who should I say called?

Man: This is Bill Jackson. I'll call her back this evening.

178.   *Woman:*   Hello.

        Man: Hello. Is Bob at home?

    Woman: No, he isn't. May I take a message?

        Man: Yes. Tell him George called.

179.   *Woman:*   Hilton Hotel. May I help you?

        Man: Mr. John Thomas. Room 213 please.

    Woman: I'll connect you. Mr. Thomas isn't in at the moment.

        Man: May I leave a message?

    Woman: Certainly. What is the message?

        Man: Have him call Alex Green at 273-7928. It's important.

180.   *Man:*   Hello.

    Woman: Is Mary at home?

        Man: No, she isn't. Can I take a message?

    Woman: Please. This is Natalie Henderson. Could you ask her to call me?

        Man: Sure. Does she have your number?

    Woman: I don't know. Maybe you'd better write it down. It's 773-5641.

B. Getting Information

181.   *Woman:*   Information. May I help you?

        Man: Yes. I'm having trouble calling the Bookshelf Bookstore.

    Woman: What number are you dialing?

        Man: 482-9736.

    Woman: Sir, the number has been changed to 978-8226.

182.   *Man:*   Information. Operator number thirteen. Can I help you?

    Woman: Can you give me the number of Ace Car Rental in Phoenix?

        Man: Just a moment please. That number is 834-2170.

    Woman: 2170. OK. Thank you.

183. *Woman:* Information. What city please?

    Man: Bakersfield

    Woman: What number do you need?

    Man: I need the number of Bill Jackson, J-A-C-K-S-O-N. He lives on Market Street.

    Woman: Did you say Bill Jackson or Gill Jackson?

    Man: Bill. That's "B" as in "boy."

    Woman: The number is 761-4688.

184. *Man:* Information. Operator 37.

    Woman: Do you have a listing for Sam Johnson?

    Man: Do you know the address?

    Woman: I believe he lives on Parkway Boulevard.

    Man: I'm sorry. We don't have a Sam Johnson on Parkway.

185. *Man-1:* Information. What number do you need?

    Man-2: I need the number of the German Embassy in Los Angeles.

    Man-1: You'll have to dial information in Los Angeles. Dial 1-213-555-1212.

    Man-2: Right. Thanks.

C. Long Distance Calls

186. *Man:* Hello.

    Operator: I have a collect call from Pedro Salazar. Will you accept the charges?

    Man: Sure. Put him on.

187. *Operator:* Operator.

    Woman: Operator, I'm trying to call 274-1347.

    Operator: That number is outside of this zone. It's a dollar thirty for three minutes.

    Woman: All right. I'll put in the coins.

188. *Operator:* Overseas Operator. Which country?

     Man: Iran.

     Operator: Yes, go ahead.

     Man: I'd like to book a call to Tehran, Iran.

     Operator: For which date and time?

     Man: March twenty-first at three p.m.

     Operator: What's your name and phone number?

     Man: Mike James 964-5397. The number in Iran is 827-803.

     Operator: We'll call you when your call is ready to go through.

189 *Operator:* Overseas Operator.

     Woman: I'd like to place a call to France.

     Operator: Your number please?

     Woman: Area code 513, number 433-5009.

     Operator: Which city in France?

     Woman: Paris. The number is 924896.

     Operator: Your call is ready. Go ahead.

D. Wrong Numbers and Unwanted Calls

190. *Man:* Hello.

     Woman: Hello. May I speak to Jim?

     Man: I'm afraid you have the wrong number.

     Woman: Isn't this 278-2001?

     Man: No, this is 278-2010.

191. *Woman:* Hello.

     Man: Hello. Is Bob in?

     Woman: There's no Bob here. What number are you dialing?

     Man: I'm trying to reach Robert Brown at 789-8307.

     Woman: That's our number, but you've made a mistake. Maybe you'd better check his listing again.

     Man: I'll do that. Sorry for disturbing you.

192. **Woman:** Hello. Cowden residence.

    Man: Is this Mrs. Cowden?

    Woman: Yes, it is.

    Man: Mrs. Cowden, I represent a company with a fine line of household cleansers and our company representative will be in your neighborhood soon and we'd like to stop by to show . . . .

    Woman: I'm sorry. I'm afraid I already have all the cleansers I need.

193. **Man:** Hello.

    Woman: Hello. Is this the Jackson residence?

    Man: Yes, it is . . .

    Woman: We understand that you've recently purchased a home.

    Man: That's correct.

    Woman: Well, Mr. Jackson, I represent the Acme Water Purification System Company, and as you know . . . .

    Man: I'm sorry. I'm not interested.

12. Making Excuses

194. **Woman:** You didn't call me last night, did you?

    Man: Yes. I called several times but you didn't answer.

    Woman: I was home all night. You must have dialed the wrong number.

195. **Woman:** Bob, where were you yesterday? We had a meeting.

    Man: Was I supposed to come to the meeting?

    Woman: Yes. The meeting was for the entire group.

    Man: Oh, I'm sorry. I didn't know that.

196. **Man:** Hi, honey.

    Woman: Where have you been? It's nine o'clock already.

    Man: I had to work late tonight.

    Woman: Well, you should have called me.

197. Man-1: Have you finished typing that report for me?

      Man-2: Not yet.

      Man-1: But I gave it to you yesterday morning.

      Man-2: I know, but I've been very busy.

198. Woman: Why are you so late?

      Man: I had a flat tire on the way over here.

      Woman: But the party's almost over.

      Man: Oh, that's too bad. Is there any foot left?

199. Woman-1: Meyers Cotton Company.

      Woman-2: Miss Davis, this is Jean Thompson. I can't come in to work for a couple of days.

      Woman-1: What's the problem? Are you sick?

      Woman-2: No. My grandmother died and I have to go out of town for the funeral.

200. Man-1: How about coming over to our place for dinner this weekend?

      Man-2: Friday or Saturday?

      Man-1: How is Saturday night around seven or so?

      Man-2: Oh, no. We already have plans for Saturday.